Will the Real Pakistani Woman Please Stand Up?

Will the Real Pakistani Woman Please Stand Up?

Empire, Visual Culture and the Brown Female Body

MOON CHARANIA

McFarland & Company, Inc., Publishers
Jefferson, North Carolina

LIBRARY OF CONGRESS CATALOGUING-IN-PUBLICATION DATA

Charania, Moon, 1976–
　　Will the real Pakistani woman please stand up? : empire, visual culture and the brown female body / Moon Charania.
　　　　p.　　cm.
　　Includes bibliographical references and index.

　　ISBN 978-0-7864-9999-1 (softcover : acid free paper) ∞
　　ISBN 978-1-4766-2250-7 (ebook)

　　1. Women—Pakistan.　2. Muslim women—Pakistan. 3. Human body—Social aspects—Pakistan.　4. Feminism—Pakistan.　5. Visual sociology—Pakistan.　I. Title.
　　HQ1745.5.C48　2015
　　305.4095491—dc23　　　　　　　　　　　　　　2015030196

BRITISH LIBRARY CATALOGUING DATA ARE AVAILABLE

© 2015 Moon Charania. All rights reserved

No part of this book may be reproduced or transmitted in any form or by any means, electronic or mechanical, including photocopying or recording, or by any information storage and retrieval system, without permission in writing from the publisher.

Cover image © Zurijeta/Thinkstock

Printed in the United States of America

McFarland & Company, Inc., Publishers
　Box 611, Jefferson, North Carolina 28640
　　www.mcfarlandpub.com

For my mother … who gifted me the intimacy of my Pakistani-ness, weaving into my crevices the lines of nation(s), while simultaneously mocking all nationalisms as nothing more than overly played out, passionate masculine parodies

Table of Contents

Acknowledgments   ix
Preface   1

One. Vision as Violence: An Introduction   7

Two. Paranoid Archives: Pakistan in the Field of Visuality, War and Empire   27

Three. Fetish, Fantasy and Freedom: Brown Women's Bodies as Subject of/to Human Rights   41

Four. Is There a Queer Democracy? Or—Stop Looking Straight: Benazir Bhutto and the Hetero-Erotics of Democracy   71

Five. "Chicks with Sticks": Pleasure, Subversion and Insubordination in Female Political Subjectivity in Pakistan   108

Coda. Will the Real Pakistani Woman Please Stand Up? Unhappy Archives and the Failure of Visual Culture   121

Chapter Notes   137
Bibliography   141
Index   147

Acknowledgments

This book has been a long journey, and the people who have traversed this road with me have been varied and many. There have been a number of feminist spirits for me in the academy, all of whom have offered their unwavering belief in the importance of this project and have extended genuine solidarity. I am grateful for the feminist and antiracist politics of hope these important scholars bring to my work but even more importantly to these perilous times of empire building.

The early formations of this book came into being through conversations with Dr. Chet Meeks, whose brilliance and wit and impatience with my stumbling critiques strengthened my ideas, compelled me into nuance and invigorated my love for intellectual possibility. His death in 2008 catalyzed a series a changes in my life, changes that perhaps would have taken much longer to materialize and I am so grateful for the ways he taught me that it is not just life, but death and departure, that also open up possibility. Chet challenged my intellectual imagination, and in so doing, released my own complex imaginaries. Wendy Simond's friendship has been integral to me since I entered the academy. Our friendship was in part catalyzed by the death of our dear and brilliant friend and colleague Chet Meeks. But I was drawn to Wendy from the minute I met her for her radical, unapologetic feminism, her refusal to participate in the hierarchy of the academy, her sharp mind and her humor. She has played many a role in my life, as sister, friend, wedding crasher, mentor, editor, and family member—and for each crossing, each trans-

Acknowledgments

gression, every piece of advice, and endless readings, I am eternally grateful.

A short and thematic-centered version of Chapter 5 appeared in *Border Politics: Social Movements, Collective Identities and Globalization* (New York University Press, 2014). I want to thank Nancy Naples for inviting me to this fantastic collection very early in my career and for believing in my work, despite the challenges, and Jennifer Mendez, who I came to know through *Border Politics*, and who cast a loving and critical eye on my work, refining my essay and my thoughts. My deepest thanks to all those who listen to me endlessly talk about this project: Christina Barmon, Cory Albertson, Ann Pollack, Nancy Maveety, Heidi Hoechst, Elizabeth Beck, Susan Talburt and Danielle Egan—all of whom extended themselves in innumerable ways to support my work.

Writing anything, much less a book, with a young child is challenging beyond words. Thus, the hours of writing were all the more precious because they were often difficult to come by. I could not have come this far without the love and support of my family, who stepped up in every possible way, offering me precious minutes, hours and sometimes days to immerse myself in this project. A special gratitude is reserved for my mother, who raised me with a fantastic blend of cynicism as well as a deep belief in humanity, even when her own life circumstances made the latter trying. My mother has graciously endured and curiously supported me during this journey, even when my choices transformed her life in difficult ways.

I owe many lifetimes of sheer gratitude to Amin, without whom all the pragmatics of a life filled with writing would not have come to fruition. My dear cousin and more so, fellow feminist sojourner, Sara Shroff, has unfailingly provided me with valuable feedback, enthusiasm and support, even when I faltered. I always look fondly at our afternoons (and late nights) filled with lively conversations. And, to Erin, who never stopped for one minute believing in this project, no matter the hardships that came our way. She has held my hand and my heart throughout this long winter. And last but not least, there would be no book if it were not for my *gurya*, Zoya. You have brought beauty and wisdom into my life from the minute you entered this world. Everything I do is for you and because of you.

Preface

Pakistan leaves its psychic print on me, intense, unforgiving, tender. A deep nostalgia runs through me daily, but its distance stretches out in front of me. Water, land, war, death and politics announce the disappearance of the Pakistan I knew. Its veracity lingers only in the memories of those who lived it and in the complex truths of those who continue to occupy it.

If nations are constituted by relations of desire and familiarity, community and connectivity, imagined solidarities and real practices of eating and speaking, sights and smells, clothes and music and poetry, then perhaps I never left Pakistan. But indeed I did. When I left Pakistan, I was too young to understand why my mother cogently gathered all these things close, how my father's refusal to allow us to speak English in the house erected a wall that kept us from ever assimilating into (the whiteness of) America, and how the dreams that connected them to the route back banished with time and space. Instead, I left with the arrogance of young girl who thought returning to the past was as simple as returning to a country. I didn't know, then, that time would and could dilute the "Pakistani" in me. I was, of course, naïve. America, as my mother would say, was both a benediction and a curse.

But if I can find Pakistan at all, I must first acknowledge that it does not exist. I might have once believed from the Badshahi masjid of Lahore to the winding roads of Chitral to the coastline of my hometown, Karachi, that its borders were solid. Now I know otherwise. And though I would never dispense of it, I admit that Pakistan is itself a metaphor. Metaphors no more imagined or constructed than national and regional borders depend upon perspective. In this way, then, my book is charged with my sound existential desire to remain connected to Pakistan—my family's crisscrossing of Shiite traditions with 70s and 80s Karachi urbanism, my mother tongue, *Urdu,* the fragility and precariousness of the grand collective *we* Pakistanis feel, and perhaps some artificial but inevitable nostalgia around the cultural, aesthetic and political habitus that shaped and continues to shape my and my daughter's life. I am, frankly, embedded in my subject, but perhaps not strikingly different than the way any feminist writer is embedded in "woman," a postcolonialist in the subaltern, a critical race scholar in the politics of race.

Images of women define the borders of my journey, within and outside Pakistan. And images of Pakistani women arrest the contemporary cultural imagination, as brown bodies become capital in the formations of benevolent white multiculturalism. This book is about these images of women and the visual cultural cycle that relies on the repetition, familiarity and ideology of these visualized subjects. The familiar public spectacles of racialized and feminized oppression, the diva citizenship of Anglicized Muslim women, and the embodied Islamized terrorist are fraught with claims of U.S. exceptionalism and racial romanticism. These women are Muslim in a time where Muslim is no longer (if it ever was) a model minority. Instead these women, and representations of them, are incredibly freighted and fragmented as both heroines of oppression and mata haris, whereby both emerge and are submerged in a mess of images around Muslim masculinity, global political schemata, and a pantheon of stereotypes. Saadiya Haartman (2007:174–175) tells us, "In Western philosophy, knowledge has been conceived as primarily an ocular function. To know is to see, to see is the inception of thought. The mind has been described as an inner eye and knowledge as a series of visual perceptions or pictures. Sight is the sense elevated above all others in apprehending the world" (Haartman 174–175). Indeed, the serious investigation of visual signs in the experience of colonialism has only recently begun (Landau and Kaspin 2002, McClintock 1998). As Paul Landau and Deborah Kaspin (2002) argue, images have long played a critical, if largely unexamined, role—mediating relationships between the colonizer and the colonized, the state and the individual, and the global and the local.

In the past decade, the archive of both visual and textual Pakistan

Preface

has indeed grown but the image—Pakistan—has become flatter and simpler in its resonances. Frankly, images of Pakistan can never be addressed on their own terms since those terms don't readily present themselves and dense clusters of meanings are obscured in the service of simple and accessible epistemologies of the *other*. For the most part I am interested in the subjective formation of s/he who looks at Pakistani women rather than s/he who is looked at. Thus this project is limited to the politics of representation and the epistemologies, real and phatasmic, which visuality enacts. It is not a project that maps the subjectivity of these women. From my standpoint, I can only gather from their words (written by them, written on them) the subjective possibilities that they may open up. In this way, this book, perhaps more than being about Pakistan or Pakistani women, insofar as neither of these has any ontological stability, is fundamentally about the power, pleasure and politics of representing Pakistan in the war-torn transnational field—a field in which Pakistan daily comes to be a more and more complicated site.

As a queer woman of color, a woman of Pakistani descent, writing and living in the United States, my diasporic consciousness and research embeds me in my subject even as it creates tension with the pursuit of the *other*, marking my project with disaffections, ruptures and incomprehensions. Skepticism, criticality and a respect for the integrity of difference, replaces the research goal of total understanding and representation. Hence, my account of these Pakistani feminine/feminist fields is at odds with (any) patriotic/imperialist nationalism and deconstructive of Western categories of analysis. Gayatri Spivak (1988) frames the deconstructive position as saying an impossible *no* to a structure that one critiques, yet nevertheless inhabits intimately, in my case, through simultaneous levels of sociological knowing, teaching and writing in the American academy.

Since I write as a feminist researcher and postmodern critic, neither the correctness of representation nor its fidelity to some original form of the real Pakistani woman are my goals. Instead, as my title suggests, this very relationship between the gendered nationalist subject and visual culture is theatrical in its attempt to represent Pakistan "as it is" and often leaves us with an extraordinary restriction of the relations of power through which any such figure is imagined or emerges. Pakistan and the oft-cited figure of the Pakistani woman is one that is made obscure, darkened by and through visual technology, here, the camera that claims to narrate her subjecthood to the vested audience of the West. In asking the "real" Pakistani woman to please stand up, this book troubles, indeed queers, the sentimentality attached to notions of nation and woman, but also more broadly concepts of authenticity, visibility and representation.

To get at this, I examine the visual and linguistic texts that have proliferated around "the Pakistani woman"—a discursively produced subject who is rooted in particular structures of narration and modes of intelligibility. This renovation of the Pakistani woman and her connotations, is what Michel Foucault (1977) calls a *discursive formation*—a systematic dispersion of statements across various fields. In newspapers, official reports, political debates, literary and visual representations and social commentary, we can locate multiple surfaces where Pakistan and the Pakistani woman has emerged as subject par intrigue. Hence, the images and texts I deconstruct must be seen as both real and imagined, a Deleuzian and Gauttarian (1988) becoming and a formation, incomplete and a totality. This is not to advocate a postmodern fetishization of incoherence or fragmentation of the subject. Instead, I struggle to situate these visual subjects (and myself as yet again authoring these subjects), outside of the binary frames within which they are narrated and within the heteroglossia of political instability, wartime urgency, and modernist telos wherein their subject-hood becomes intriguing, entertaining and concretized.

Had not the women enfolded in these pages braved the daggers of cultural misogyny, paranoid empires and national sedimentation, perhaps I would not have a story to tell on Pakistani women, transnational feminist labor and the U.S. state/gaze. I am separated from these women not just by lines drawn in land, but by class and culture, by life and death. In my search for understanding, I can only hope that I have not missed understandings. And so, I re-author these women with equal degrees of nostalgia and irony. I regard my gesture, as James Clifford (1988:9) puts it, "as a state of being in culture while looking at culture." In this way, I want to take care to avoid making my own position seem either paradigmatic or normative. I recognize that other researchers in my position (woman of color, immigrant, living in the U.S.) do not share my critical view of U.S. imperialism and its reflection in gendered images. From Frantz Fanon's (1963) theorization of race and colonialism to the Anne Cheng's (2000) work on race and melancholy, my argument is buttressed with rigorous re-readings of racial theory and feminism. I draw from a variety of disciplines, feminist studies, postcolonial studies, and visual cultural studies to illuminate the "strange" "queer" and "disturbed" relationships, questions, and entanglements that these visual moments foster and provoke.

Each chapter focuses on a set of visual images or an image around a particular visual subject as they were deployed in their varying contexts of apprehension or intrigue. I show how, ironically, the ascendency of the hetero-patriarchal, paranoid gaze, in varying degrees with varying permutations, both reproduces the rampant exploitation and/or cooptation of these Pakistani women but also paradoxically compels a queer theoretical labor, one that links violence to liberal deployments of diversity and the valorization of life. Using different socio-cultural registers to read female bodies imbricated in various postcolonial predicaments, I underscore the affect, pleasure and the erotic embedded within these women's representations. As the reader moves through the varying photographed and narrated fields of Pakistan, you will see that I analyze each photograph and text for what social modalities it allows, organizes, elides, and constrains. Each chapter exposes how the erotic becomes palpable through queer re-readings of the dominant gaze to result in different degrees of domination and discipline imposed over these women subjects. I stress, through each photograph, the violence of visuality, the patterns of domination and subordination through which these images have vacillated, and the hetero-erotic gaze that has been recuperated through them. I blend visual research, discourse analysis, and my own implications in these women's life, death and feminist politics which, I hope, allows the reader both theoretical depth and accessibility. I hope to encourage readers to think deeply about what photographs of feminine, racialized subjects mean and how so much of those meanings are interpreted through their gender bodies and sexualized aesthetics.

One

Vision as Violence
An Introduction

Vision is always a question of the power to see—and perhaps of the violence implicit in our visualizing practices. With whose blood were my eyes crafted?

—Donna Haraway (1991:585)

In the summer of 2010, fans worldwide deliriously enjoyed the much-anticipated *Sex and the City 2 (SATC2)*. Generating almost half a billion dollars, *SATC2* pivots around the four New York women's experience in the "Middle East," where Carrie (the central character of the series, and then later, the films) anticipates "desert moons, Scheherazade, magic carpets." In a key climactic scene of the blockbuster movie *Sex and the City 2,* the intrepid Manhattan foursome of Carrie, Miranda, Charlotte and Samantha take safe harbor in a mysterious, incense-shrouded chamber of veiled, Abu Dhabi women. The veiled women give refuge to the *Sex and the City* crew women after Samantha spills dozens of condoms from her purse in the middle of a spice market crowded with men. The men, overwhelmed by anger and shock, abandon their daily activities and busy life to encircle Samantha and condemn her as a harlot, leading to a confrontation between the four women and dozens of angry men in the Abu Dhabi marketplace. Mocking their indignation, Samantha proudly holds the condoms up high, her cleavage pouring out, and dry humps the air, yelling, "Yes, I have sex!" The other three women, looking

Will the Real Pakistani Woman Please Stand Up?

on with exasperation and fear, pull Samantha away from the screaming Arab men surrounding them. The scene slows down only as the women just barely escape the crowds of men when two mysterious veiled[1] women appear, silently nodding to the four women as an invitation. Our four cultural avatars follow the mere gaze (and nod) into a private space, reminiscent of an Urdu *zenana*,[2] where the women of Abu Dhabi reveal the existence of a secret club attended by a dozen *niqabi*[3] women. The foursome's initial trepidation—even aversion—towards these veiled/oppressed women dissolves as the women drop their veils to reveal the same high-end Western couture that hang from the shoulders of our emancipated American foursome. Carrie, recognizing the threads of French designer Louis Vuitton, wittingly states, "Under hundreds of years of tradition, was this year's spring collection!"

The final shot of America's favorite feminine/feminist fantasy scene lights up with the intermeshed sounds of all the women laughing at what *Salon* magazine glibly calls "sexisms' funeral" (Ali 2010). It's a scene that's supremely unrealistic, woefully incongruous and purely pleasurable as

Figure 1. *Sex and the City 2*, 2010, desert scene. From left to right: Kim Cattrall, Kristin Davis, Sarah Jessica Parker, Cynthia Nixon.

One. Vision as Violence

it brings together *burqas* and *haute couture*. The message of the scene is tremendously appealing among American liberals and self-defined social progressives, as the film turns hard-won sexual rights and gender equality into badges of national honor and patriotic pride. Actually, more than three quarters of the film takes place in Abu Dhabi (though it was filmed in Morocco) and is replete with mockeries of veiled women and Muslim men, what *Salon* magazine's Wajahat Ali (2010) identifies as "stunning Muslim clichés."

This cinematic representation of Muslim women, in a number of ways, while more than faintly ridiculous, is reminiscent of orientalists' caricatures and occidental self-congratulatory schemata. Authorized, at least in part, by the contemporary geopolitical realities that have propelled Muslim women (and men) into the global gaze, the message(s) of the underlined "us" and "they" is clear: we are the (white) liberated Americans and they are the oppressed (brown) women. The sharing of space and coutured bodies by both the brown and white women operates as a disavowal of the films' racist undertones, but the formula through which we have come to gaze at the Muslim woman, and her liberated American counterpart, is nonetheless strikingly transparent in this interface of power and pleasure.

The scene, itself, constructed through the (dangerous) incident in the bazaar and the (securitizing) moment in the *zenana*, incites an intrigue around Muslim bodies and subjects, vacillating between representations of danger to oppression to liberation, and the sexualization of all three. Indeed, at each level of the scene we see how the erotic continues to provoke paranoia and pleasure, often simultaneously, and always through the Muslim fe/male body. The scene illustrates how the female racialized body, here the *niqabi* Muslim women, is irrevocably intertwined with discourses of perfected femininity that wrap white woman subjects in discursive adornments such as (faux) feminism, modernity, and consumption of the *other*. For Carrie and for the audience of *SATC2*, the very act of disrobing these black shrouds of fabric is a step toward their emancipation, or "sexism's funeral." The act appears to reference a sexual economy of secrecy and disclosure, a promise of the erotic that underlies the *niqab*, waiting to be uncovered (Gopinath 2005). The scene's self-congratulatory tone as having conquered sexism implies that feminism/femininity is always and already present among white women, seductively condensing feminism to specific feminine embodiments, such as skimpily dressed women as liberated and access to haute couture as empowerment.

Will the Real Pakistani Woman Please Stand Up?

But this climactic scene also confounds the erotic because it uses a dominant registrar of visibility, women removing their clothes, to frame another economy of desire and pleasure rooted in seeing the *other* as ourselves. When Carrie excitedly gasps in joy at the site of the *niqabi* women in familiar European couture, she unwittingly elucidates how the construction of the *other* serves as a vantage point from which to observe the self. This scene interpellates a Western viewing public that is literate in all these referenced codes: the oppressed Muslim woman, the veil and the veiled as fearful, the erotic underlay of removing the veil to reveal a sexualized, racialized female *other*, and this *other* being/becoming "like us." The dynamics of power and constrain that contour the book club scene (indeed, they are reading the same book that menopausal Samantha cites the entire film) give way to the celebratory ethos of ordinary (white) women who create their seemingly autonomous pleasures and rituals of enjoyable femininity from the goods made available by consumer culture—now a practice made available to ordinary (Muslim) women who, too, can participate in gendered consumer culture as an act of sexual power. In *SATC2*, we find ourselves dealing with an old racial and imperial problematic now enacted through popular visual culture—white liberal feminist production of agency (and particular definition of freedom and modernity) for itself by the way it figures the Muslim woman as oppressed and veiled, or when unveiled, claiming consumer global modernities through haute couture. Ultimately, this scene annexes the whole décor of Muslim culture into merely a *trompe l'oeil* visual universe in which all the particularities of nation, religion and sex can become parodies of themselves or can be cast off to reveal we are all one and the same.

Adding to the weight of collective visual instruction is the complex historical and contemporary tensions between the U.S. and a number of Muslim nations. The *SATC2* scene fastens this discursive tension. The bustling market disrupted by the visual display of (white, female) sexuality and (Muslim, male) violence demonstrates anxieties about the inevitability of brown men's violence. The specific cinematic strategy of falling condoms, scantily dressed Samantha bending down to pick up the condoms, and large numbers of brown men encircling the four white women bespeaks the possibility of a gang rape, even as it caricaturizes it. Even in the *zenana*-like space, the barbarism of the Muslim male is both incited and mocked, as these women demonstrate, through the revelation of skimpy couture beneath the veil, that angry brown men can be out-

One. Vision as Violence

witted. Once Muslim women slip seamlessly into the empowered space of the liberal feminist project, all women can bond over despising angry, oppressive and dangerous brown Muslim men.

In the above popularized still from *SATC2* (**fig. 1**), the U.S. freedom avatars stroll through the Sahara in Abu Dhabian silks. **Fig. 1**, in all its visual excitement of white women crossing national, erotic and aesthetic borders, illustrates the crisscrossing articulations of Western feminine aesthetics and erotics with the exotic palatability of *otherness,* where both come to signify the visual face of feminist emancipation. The photographic still references an orientalist spatiality of sand dunes, deserts and sexy and sexually available (brown) women. But in situating the white foursome in this exotic space, wearing garments from these faraway lands, the visuality evokes a fantasied site of erotic and imperial play. The bright colors, the long hair, the jewelry, the display of cleavage, all elicit a fetishistic response from the viewer, naturalizing the hetero-erotic and the imperial gaze. Or as Theresa de Lauretis (1993) argues, the representation of women as spectacle—a body to be looked at, a place of sexuality, and object of desire—so pervasive in our culture finds in narrative cinema its most complex expression and widest circulation. From the excited brown men of the market scene to the disrobing women of the *zenana* to the erotic aesthetics of white women donning "Arab" silks, this representation reveals a subtle subterfuge of pleasure associated with such fetishized visualities of Muslim women.

The story of imperial legacies, (colonial) empires and their fetishes is undoubted familiar. But after 9/11, the invasion of Iraq (and the recent recession from Iraq), Afghanistan and Pakistan, the imperial impulse to make visible the "barbarisms" of the global south is especially pervasive. For example, in the 18 months following 9/11, there was a sixfold increase in the number of newspaper articles focusing on women in Afghanistan (Stabile & Kumar, 2005), and the articles include descriptions of burqas as body bags and trash bags. This burgeoning fascination has propelled both Muslim women and men into the global gaze prompting representation in mainstream magazines, press, and coffee-table books and seeping into public cultural and political discourse, through the mediums of stories, photographs, sensationalized events and figures, documentaries and cinema. However, this popularity of Muslim women must be contextualized within the current socio-political landscape, where heightened anxieties toward Islam, Muslims and Arabs is prevalent; where increased surveillance, detention and violence against this community is legitimated in the name of security; where foreign policy coupled with military measures are deployed to remap countries; and where "saving" Muslim women is a priority both within and outside of visual culture.

The *SATC2* scene animates a cultural landscape and an epistemological process that simultaneously seeks and produces nativized fetishes and feminized fetishes at the nexus of geopolitical histories of desire for the *other* and exploitation of the *other*. While *SATC2* is not necessarily related to Pakistan, the film—like the visual fields I analyze—is organized around the (nationalized patriarchal) dilemmas the emancipated, white foursome face in the sexually repressed, dangerous Muslim world, ostensibly juxtaposing scene after scene the oppression of brown/Muslim women and the freedom of our white/American women. The blockbuster film, *Sex and the City 2*, shows how unveiling the Muslim woman both literally and metaphorically has been a fantasy and a mission taken on by both the white racial state and liberal feminist women. Even a cursory look at *SATC2's* popularized still reveals the ways (white) women have been appropriated as a tangible means of solidifying Western heteronationalisms, modernity, and war. The confluence of similarity between Hollywood's entertaining representation of Emirati Muslim women versus the documentary nature of the Pakistani women's photographs that occupy the pages of this book is striking—oscillating, like the film, between dangerous gender oppression to liberated feminine/feminist aesthetics to an eroticized removal of the veil (in the service of empire). By opening with the polemical, visually—oriented cinematic moment of *SATC2*, a film that incites and eases U.S. intrigue in the Muslim *other* primarily through the display of Emirate-Muslim women, this book proposes that visual culture emerging out of or around Pakistan enables a set of discourses through which racial formations around Muslim women and the Pakistani nation-state are constituted and exercised.

Will the Real Pakistani Woman Please Stand Up? is situated at the convergence of conversations on visual culture, the white racial state and the semiotics of empire. Using Pakistan as my point of entry, I critically document and interrogate the dramatic visual intrigue around Muslim and/or brown women's bodies and subjectivities since 9/11. I use transnationally traversed, Pakistani cultural stories, events and figures as an entry point for mapping the visual and spectacular aspects of the neocolonial condition. I consider three primary visual fields, but also significant secondary representations, that operate as snapshots of Pakistani women, and Muslim women more broadly, after September 11, 2001:

One. Vision as Violence

international human rights sensation Mukhtar Mai and other human rights figures celebrated by U.S. liberal feminist events/outlets; twice elected Prime Minister of Pakistan and first woman to lead a Muslim country Benazir Bhutto; and female terrorists/religious martyrs[4] of the 2007 Red Mosque events in Islamabad, Pakistan. I locate the relevance of these visual stories on three axes: human rights, democratization, and the war on terror, where each operates as an arm of the U.S. "heteronormative nation" (Puar 2007: xxv).

While I draw on the nuances of Pakistan's geopolitical location in the global war and the U.S. heteronormative state's contemporary practices in the regions of Pakistan, Afghanistan and Iraq, this book is less about Pakistan and more about the postcolonial—or rather, neocolonial—condition. I use Pakistan, and more specifically Pakistani women, to direct a critical gaze towards photography and towards the systems that use visual practice to name themselves as free and identify the *other* as dangerous or desirable (a point we see quite lucidly in *SATC2*). By centering my analysis on the linguistic styles, figures of speech, narrative devices, and visual tropes deployed to *see*/constitute these women, I work to answer a number of questions. What discourses are central to these visual and rhetorical fields? What are the functions of these discourses? How do these visual stories operate as central sites of spectatorship? In what ways do these images serve as sites of social and psychic satisfaction? What effects do these representations, shifting and uneven as they are, in the U.S. and elsewhere, have on notions of human rights, democracy, war and peace?

In approaching photographs and narrativizations of sensationalized Pakistani women as the objects of criticism, I interrogate the structures of affect, pleasure and eroticism that are embedded in these popularized representations and narrations in the U.S. cultural context. In this regard, I examine the ways sexuality, and its varying components of pleasure and affect, is situated as an integral and integrated diagrammatic vector of power in these visual fields. I elucidate the ways in which these global visual subjects are reduced to an object of the heterosexual fe/male gaze, analyzing the epistemological foundation that supports the ways in which they are *seen* and the logic that positions feminine/feminist *others* into bifurcated categories of oppressed or free specularity, where the possibility of both are read through the landscape of the female body. Using democracy, human rights and the global war as my three axes, I work through the effects of three of the most pernicious legacies of colonization—the production

Will the Real Pakistani Woman Please Stand Up?

/reverence of the victim cum feminist subject, the vacuity of liberatory political enterprise and the subtle violent erotics that constructs the feminine, racialized *other*—to demonstrate how they serve as the base for postcolonial forms of patriarchal control. Reworking, then, earlier intellectual articulations of colonial politics where *woman* was read as the invisible subject, I argue instead that the hypervisibility of brown/Muslim women's bodies in the global war posits the Muslim woman as the paradigmatic citizen of Empire. I thread together key cultural practices (like visibility, voice and story–telling on/of the *other*) to explain how these embodied subjects are made to function according to complementary U.S. narrations of human rights, democracy and war. By bringing together disparate contemporary cultural and political subjects of Pakistan within a single analytic framework of the *feminine, racialized other,* I examine the desire to erotically *see/consume* the *other*. The photographic narratives of these Pakistani women reveals that contemporary formations/ transmutation of democracy, terror and freedom are, in fact, laced with a hetero-erotic desire for the (brown) female *other* as well as a homoerotic dread of the (brown) male *other*.

As you move through these visual fields, you will note that I interchangeably use the terms brown women and Muslim women. I do this not to imply that they are synonymous neither do I argue that Muslim/ Pakistani/brown woman as a representational equation is THE dominant representation mode. Obviously, Muslim/Pakistani is not the same as Muslim/Arab, in terms of specific representations, although I will present a seamless arc in which all types of Muslim-ness are placed. The co-construction of brown and Muslim is key to the intersectional and simultaneous politics of difference and representation that I analyze throughout the book, recognizing that all forms of racialization are fraught with complexity and ambiguity by both the racialized subjects themselves and the dominating gaze. Given my interest in excavating U.S. race-based constructions of particular exotic/erotic/racial subjectivity, this co-relation is utilized to frame my discussion of these female subjects within the broader racialization of Islam that we've seen since the events of 9/11 (Grewal 2005; Puar 2007; McClintock 2009). The Pakistani visual figures I examine exemplify racial distinctions within the U.S. while simultaneously opening up possibilities for queering the complex, imperialist national formations that shape contemporary politics. The racialized and sexualized ideologies that undergird the transnational proliferation of photographs of the *other* is imbricated in various postcolonial predicaments—the politics of visibility, feminism as an aesthetics, visual production of the *other*, eroticized nationalism and erotic empires. I look *awry* at these visualities, to queer ways of seeing the Pakistani feminine/feminist subject, the iconoclastic utility of her body, and her visual and discursive constitution as simultaneously or alternatively celebrated, grievable, monstrous, or malleable.

Visual Culture and/as Power

The saturation of social space by the visual has spawned an increasing interest in scholars, developing innovative methodologies within the context of rapid technological change. While visual research is methodologically and theoretically diverse—there is no single common heritage, aim, or defining system of analysis—there are a number of important strands of influence in the development of visual methodologies. The recent turn to the visual has unearthed a multiplicity of new problems, research questions and agendas which signal a shift in the importance of the visual in knowledge creation and extend far beyond the boundaries of scholarly disciplines. Indeed, as Stuart Hall (1990:20) alluded to, "cultural studies is not one thing, it has never been one thing." Instead, cultural studies is an adaptation to its terrain—a conjectural practice.

As a cultural studies project, a key ambition of this book is to call attention to the textuality of a paranoid imperialism and the politics of representation that claim to tell the story of the real Pakistani woman, and more broadly, the Muslim woman. The central intellectual, political and radical frames for this project are the visual constructions of feminine and feminist subjectivities, significations and transmutations of the (brown) female body, and the pleasures and paranoia's of Empire's visual culture. Edward Said (1979) argues that critical analysis should refute the merely cultural approach that views images and photographs as relatively autonomous or existing in a super-structural relationship to the political, economic and social spheres. He (1979:39) states, to ignore or dismiss the cultural terrain in which "the colonizer and colonized coexisted and battled each other through projections as well as rival geographies, narratives and histories … is to miss the massively knotted and complex histories" of colonizer and colonized. Visual scholars have well established that particular forms of representations are important to understand because they are intimately bound into social power relations

Will the Real Pakistani Woman Please Stand Up?

(Mulvey 1977; Rose 1998; Fanon 1968). As Michael Taussig (1999) emphasizes, representations of the *other* are never neutral. They are and always will be a political move, a social undertaking, a cultural statement, functioning simultaneously as a "phantasmic social force" and a "high-powered medium of domination" (Taussig 1999:23).

Image, as Landau and Kaspin (2002:2) tell us, "is a very forgiving word, even a promiscuous one." In its most basic sense, image means picture, whether the referent is present as an object, or simply in the mind. Thus, if we begin to think of the subject matter of this book—images of Pakistan through the landscape of the brown/Muslim fe/male body—we must first acknowledge that these images really consists of ideas associated with Pakistan, albeit ones that also embody visual components. Visual culture is political—a terrain, a space where we struggle for representations. Visual practices survey, discipline, and marginalize bodies. Both discourse and visuality function as mechanisms of power for constituting and disciplining (racial) subjects across and within national and imperial geographies. In this way, visual culture is a transnational median of knowledge production on the Muslim/brown *other*, in ways that serve both cultural entertainment and technologies of power.

The photographs and the visual figures that I analyze were (and continue to be) politically hailed as visual evidence of Pakistani and Islamic pathologies/potentialities. If these appears a grand claim, then, at the least, we can remark on the keen interest across the U.S., in both news and popular media, in images of Pakistan's gendered reality, specifically through photographs of Pakistani women and their decided oppression (think, for example of the U.S./UK fascination with Malala Yousafzai). While it can be argued that these images may be *seen* vis-à-vis multiple gazes, both visual and discursive media portrayals rely upon what Nicholas Mirzeoff (1998:7) refers to as "a dominant global gaze." Such a gaze has been loosely defined by visual scholars, wherein the viewer engages each image within the framework proposed by the dominant visual regime—a regime conditioned by neoliberalism, heteropatriarchy, late capitalism, U.S. American hegemony, Islamophobia, and the global war. The desire to *see* these images is also compounded by and around mainstream acceptability, panoptical governance, and a heteroerotic aesthetic. In this context, the visual figures I analyze were championed as representative of a dangerous Pakistan, even if these women's actual politics or social actions refuted such simplistic categorizations.

In critiquing the grip of dominant culture on the female body and

One. Vision as Violence

the woman subject, I do not want to cast the dominant gaze as a totalizing, seamless and univocal neither do I wish to cast active and creative subjects as passive dupes of ideology. I further recognize that the weight of each image is mired in multiple and inconsistent contents and that we cannot know the full extent of their appeal. Moreover, there is also a tension in Pakistan, and more broadly Muslim societies, between people who hold competing visions of what it means to be Muslim. This tension also plays a role in substantiating the imagery as il/legitimate. So, while orientalism greatly influences the construction and popularity of visual cultural images of the Pakistani as oppressed/terrorist/exotic play, Pakistanis also have a role to play in stories that get told. But precisely because I want to get at mainstream constructions of feminine, racialized *other,* I chose iconoclastic images and stories that produce and sustain hegemonic discourses of the Pakistani/brown woman. While I recognize that intent can never really be known, the visual cultural forms that bring these women's stories into U.S. living rooms, coffee houses and boardroom can be contextualized within a range of practices and discourses that lasso gendered, raced and sexualized representations in the deployment of U.S. nationalism and empire

I use American newspapers and media, generally described as well-respected, including the *New York Times, CBC, Huffington Post, American Prospect, Time, Washington Post, Newsweek* and *National Geographic.* I look at International Press such as *BBC, Dawn, Pakistani Times, Geotv* and *All Things Pakistani.* I also look at Nicholas Kristoff and Sheryl Wudunn's widely acclaimed book, *Half the Sky: Turning Oppression into Opportunity,* as well as the film based on this book, and the posthumously released documentary on Bhutto, *Benazir Bhutto: The Film* (2010). Although I look at differ kinds of media—U.S., British, Indian and Pakistani magazines, newspapers, and editorial pieces—all of which are governed by different professional demands, political configurations, markets and audiences, I do not seek to flatten these differences but rather to demonstrate how, despite these differences, a certain ontology and epistemology are taken as axiomatic by all of them. The Empire's project of making (Pakistani) experience and subjects visible relies primarily on hegemonic premises, such as the integrity and coherence of visual regimes, the heteronormative gaze that wants to see women's bodies, and imperial presumptions that fluently equate seeing with knowing, with knowledge, and with truth. Indeed, within this discursive field, seeing *appears* less complicated.

Visuality, which refers to the conditions of how we see and make meaning of what we see, is positioned within a discursive field of power where visual sign systems are deployed to achieve certain ends. Simply, visuality is a strategy. It is neither neutral nor static. Visualities don't achieve these ends within a vacuum; rather, as I've pointed out earlier (e.g., *SATC2*), they do so within certain contexts and within the parameters of certain conditions (e.g., there must be a common set of reference points). In a Foucauldian sense, visuality is productive, disciplining and consequential. It produces, through its reiterative strategies, a subject. Once produced, it disciplines that subjectivity through varying modalities, holding consequences for the audience of this visual image and for the visual subject herself. While this may seem to presume finality, the production of a subject is an ongoing and always unfinished project, particularly when the subjects of interest are women, the very nature of the gendering process suggests imperfection, always becoming that which it can never become.

Because visualities are seen through certain matrices, or imperial norms, they may never be seen at all, except as they can be understood within a discursive system. The telling of these Pakistani women's stories, rendering these female "selves" public must be rethought as a reciprocal relation in which visibility also structures one's voice/story and what can be heard about this subject. In other words, when a subject is rendered visible, "what is made manifest and fully disclosed," as Judith Butler (2004:34) asks, depends precisely on the configurations of power in which the subject becomes visible.

Mirzoeff (1998) defines the visual subject as a person who is constituted as an agent of sight (regardless of his/her capacity to see) and also as the effect of a series of categories of visual subjectivity. The subjectivity I speak about here is not an autonomous, voluntaristic subjectivity fashioned in a protean manner. Rather, I engage a Foucauldian (1984) distinction here—the subject that is formed within the limits of a historically specific set of formative practices and moral injunctions that are delimited in advance—what Michel Foucault characterizes as "modes of subjectivation." A major strategy of this production is surveillance. In *Discipline and Punish* (1975:469), Foucault cautions, "visibility is a trap." It is through visibility, Foucault writes, that modern society exercises its controlling systems of power and knowledge. For Foucault, subjectivity is not an act of private cultivation, but rather an effect of modalities of power—power operationalized through a set of (moral)

One. Vision as Violence

discursive codes that summon an individual to constitute herself in accord with its precepts. So these visual subjects are themselves particularized in a discursive formation, by which they are, in turn, disciplined.

The persistent transnational presence and proliferation of photographs of the *other* needs to be interrogated for the ways it functions as a form of camouflage, a site of surveillance that relies on the (erotic) performance of others' violence and subjectivity. The distinction between east and west, as such like visuality, is far from neutral. The east and west are never (nor have they ever been) presented as independent geospatial attributes. The distinction between east and west is asymmetrical. The east, as Sara Ahmed (2006:14) states "has always been associated with women, sexuality and the exotic, with what is behind and below the West, as well as what is on the other side." Drawing from this, I will show how my visual subjects, quite literally, are teeming with racialized erotic codifications, determining their popularity, sensationalism, the degree of U.S. intrigue, and their place in empire.

In order to get at this, I consider the queerness embedded in both the subjects I analyze and in the modes of interpreting them to trouble and denaturalize the close relationship between hetero-eroticism, nationalism and empire. Queering these photographic landscapes of Pakistan and Pakistani women offers a different slant to the concept of global photography and visibility itself. Gayatri Gopinath (2005, 176) tells us, "queerness names a mode of reading, of rendering intelligible that which is unintelligible and indeed impossible within the dominant nationalist or imperial logic." Queerness, here, can be understood not as pertaining to sexual identity and practice, which perhaps may also be possible, but as speaking to a mode of resistant feminist cultural practice that prevents the reconstitution of patriarchal, neoliberal masculinity. In this manner, queerness disturbs the space of homeland, the notion that freedom exists outside Pakistani borders, and the singularity of the Real Pakistani nation or woman.

This disorienting experience—when we queer texts that have no gays in them—moves queerness from its primary affiliation with sexuality to a host of other possibilities and disturbing configurations. Madhavi Menon (2011:7) argues, "even as queerness is informed by its historical specificity of sexual irregularities, it cannot be reduced to or located in their embodiment." To be sure, queerness is bodily and that which challenges the limits of what can be understood as a body (of relevance, of desire, of monstrosity, and so on). Here, a central task in queering my visualities is to move away from the conflation of queer with homosexuality and stretch out the discursive field where queer theory opens up questions around affect, desire, embodiment and power. Insofar as queer theory deals with excess, queering the gaze towards the representations of these women (and more broadly, Pakistan) opens up a critical opportunity to name the excess (political, gender and sexual) that besets U.S. fears around/of Pakistan.

Queer, as Anna Marie Jagose (1998) tells us, designates a range of acts, identities, propensities, affectivities and sentiments which fissure heteronormativity." But surely this range, or as other queer theorists have called it, open up a mesh of possibilities and necessitates an openness not just to gender and sexual possibilities, but also to chronological, national, racial and philosophical choices. Even as queer theory brings all of its force to bear on questions of power, desire and sexuality, it also wants to dispense of the historical trajectory that relies on a unified, coherent subject on one hand and a chaotic, fluid subject on the other. The hypercanonical global traversal of my visual figures renders them mainstream, indeed un-queer. However, the hypercanonicity of these visual subjects also disavows the cadences through which they become visible, desirable or demonic. In this way, queering the gaze towards my visual figures moves beyond a definition of empowerment as based on free expression of identity and public visibility—key elements of a liberal-humanist didactic directed at Muslim women—and resituates the gaze to deconstruct affect, desire and power around brown bodies.

Feminine/Feminist Subjects

The categories of feminine and feminist operate as central modalities to name or un-name these subjects. In referring to the three visual fields as *feminine/feminist subjects,* I allude to the contradictory ways the female body, read as desirably feminine when engaged in tropes of normative Western feminine aesthetics (read: lipstick, uncovered hair, revealing clothing), operates as a metaphor for freedom; while the semiotic practices of brown femininity (read: *dupatta*[5] or the *niqab*) function as synecdoche for oppression. The feminine/feminist formation allows me to visually, semantically and epistemologically juxtapose readings of the ways these women are read as im/possible modern women vis-à-vis their non/normative bodies. The visual fields that I gather here speak

One. Vision as Violence

directly and indirectly to the politics of embodiment, including narratives about how bodies come to take meaning, representation of bodies varyingly dressed and undressed, and the integration of iconic glimpses into a kind of propaganda that creates an understanding of how bodies may be treated, represented, and interpreted without ever stating these as explicit injunctions. This theoretical rendering, then, works to reveal the continuum between the body as a text of femininity and the body as a site empowerment.

In a number of ways, each of the figures I analyze are constantly cast as oppressed woman first and im/possible modern subject second, with the exception of Bhutto, whom I will show came to represent, largely through the particularities of her body, the quintessential feminist Pakistani woman. My argument is that feminist subjectivity, rather than being denied or dismissed (in the Faludian anti-feminist backlash sort of way) is being instrumentalized to install a whole repertoire of new meanings and subjectivities on which the visual production of the Pakistani woman has come to rely. A prevalent thread running through this text is the discursive construction of a feminine/feminist subjectivity that frames its epistemic knowledges in highly classed and raced ways. The visualities I present are organized in silent and unobtrusive ways that allow for the illusion of empowerment—liberal-humanist project of empowerment that is seen as politically, socially or culturally neutral. For example, in chapter two, I will show how freedom is measured through Mukhtar Mai's corporeal posture and practices. These assumptions, coupled with the narrations of Benazir Bhutto as always and already free compromises feminist possibilities as they are premised on contracting oneself with certain values, aesthetics, and subjectivities. I will show that whether these figures are read or not read as feminist, democratic, modern, and so on is contingent largely on the practices of their body; a reading which anchors freedom in liberal paradigms, woman in essentialized notions of identity, and nation in racist discourses. By centering the words feminine and feminist simultaneously in my readings of these symbolic gendered fields, I want to keep taut the tension between biopolitics and liberatory politics. If biopolitics seeks directly to discipline the entirety of social life, what we see and what we imagine (to see); then liberatory politics seeks to queer that regulation, the ways we imagine freedom and *see* subjects. It is precisely within the interstices of feminine embodiment and feminist liberation that we find these brown women being folded into life, or dismissed in death, thus fueling the vacillation between the naming of populations as racialized, the disciplining of the subject as feminine, and the controlling of populations (perceived) as already free. Impelled by this folding of Pakistani female subjects into the biopolitical management of life, I work to delineate not only which brown women are (un)seen and (un)heard, but also *how* these bodies and subjects are (not) seen and (not) heard. I want to shift the optic that gazes at the Pakistani/Muslim/brown woman as a subject in need of saving (Mai) or appreciation (Bhutto) or obliteration (female martyrs) into one that understands and works against the biopolitical incitement of neoliberal/neocolonial forms of life, feminism, femininity, and most crucially, freedom.

To be sure, I articulate feminism as a network of feminist and/or freedom practices. I am not arguing that all the women I analyze are feminist. It would, for example, be a far stretch, despite the international acclamations of her as a global feminist icon, to argue that Benazir Bhutto proposed or demanded a politico-ethical stance toward understanding the ways in which all forms of culture condition or are conditioned by gender or sexual difference—much less other modes of subjectivity (such as sexuality, racial and ethnic identifications, nationality, class and so on). Neither do I argue that the martyrs of the Red Mosque, in spite of their anti-imperialist radical gendered activism, saw themselves as feminists engaged in transnational dialogues, coalitions and networks around issues of gender freedom. I recognize the critical work done around hegemonic formations of feminism, where scholars critique the common misperception that feminism originated in the West and diffused to the rest of the world. I work against the conflation of (women's) liberty with free economic action and the straitjacketing of feminism with U.S. exceptionalism and modern quality of life (Grewal 2004; Al-Ali 2000; Alexander 2005; Mohanty 2003).

But just as *SATC2* relied on the visual display of Muslim women meeting emancipation through the act of disrobing (read: disavowal of Islam), mainstream political and cultural discourses, nationally and transnationally, interpreted the visual subjects I analyze as feminine or feminist through acts of embodiment and aesthetics. Dominant framings of these Pakistani women bodies and subjectivities within context of war, democracy and human rights opens up and forecloses on interpretations on their state of freedom. I stand with other radical and decolonial thinkers who take the position that it is antithetical to the very project(s) of feminism to patrol the boundaries or map the parameters of who or

One. Vision as Violence

what is read as feminist (Al-Ali 2000; Alexander 2005). These visual fields and the subjects that occupy them stage remarkable moments of confrontation with war machines, human rights and hetero-democratic nationalisms and empires. But in each case, I will show how their visible embodiment is used to reconstruct the modern desirable subject out of their (brown) barbaric ruins.

Project Map

Heuristically speaking, each chapter in this book possesses its own analytic integrity and as such could be made to function and be read on its own. Intersecting thematics are restated under apparently different visual fields to sharpen the analytic agility with which I understand these photographs and stories. For instance, all of the chapters critique imperial practices of producing the feminine, racialized *other*, foregrounding the ideological imperatives that are deployed to function as truth or otherwise naturalize (brown) violence. I conceptualize all my visual figures as *erotic nationals*, fe/male subjects whose gender and sexual exceptionalisms and/or transgressions become points of fetishistic reproduction and disavowal by the U.S. state, a fetish implicitly but varyingly enacted and engaged through the three axes of human rights, democracy and war.

The reader will note that I often use slashes in words such as fe/male and wo/man throughout this book for a number of reasons. As I've stated, my interest in this book is at the level of the visual and, as such, how visualities of Pakistani and Muslim women and men disrupt the epistemological possibilities of them as agentic, creative and deliberate subjects. Hence, in line with my deconstruction of the visual culture that attempts to capture and colonize these women, I seek to disrupt the iconography of the language used to describe them. By slashing every use of wo/man, I confirm the psychic processes that silently evoke Muslim manhood and masculinity with every invocation of the Muslim woman. In every description of the female martyr or victim, images of the male terrorists are stirred up, incited even as they are denied. The slashing of axiomatic language allows me to convey the layers of meanings embedded in the terms, deliberately integrating that which is often regarded as disparate realities, divorced subjectivities. Moreover, just as these slashes invoke multiple meanings, they also visually disrupt the iconography of such terms—woman and female—rendering them ideologically porous and discursively fragile. Like the visual culture that seeks to represent both the Pakistani nation and woman, the language used to describe them, too, necessitates a queering—a clear and noted departure from the comforts of what has been perceived as neat translation of language (i.e., these are Urdu speaking women, a language markedly more fluid and metaphorical than English), clean analysis, and clearly marked subjectivity.

In Chapter Two, "Paranoid Archives: Pakistan in the Field of Visuality, War and Empire," I locate the relevance of Pakistan and Pakistani women and men in global visual culture. Using two widely circulated images of Pakistan, I point to the ways the Pakistani nation-state has come to be imagined through the brown fe/male body. I discuss the ways public discourse and political intrigue in Pakistan is centered around human rights victims, democratization and the nebulous role of Pakistan in the global war. Highlighting the U.S. paranoid imagination that ensnares Pakistan in a matrix of fear and jouissance, this chapter lays out the relationship between the transit of visual culture and human rights, democracy and war, where all operate as arms of the U.S. heteronormative, paranoid state.

In Chapter Three, "Fetish, Fantasy and Freedom: Brown Women's Bodies as Subject of/to Human Rights" there is a particular insight I glean from using recent Pakistani/brown women's human rights stories. The central imperative I take up in this chapter is a deconstruction of the relationship between human rights and visual culture, where the latter is lionized as a piece de resistance in a putative race-neutral rights market. As a megalomaniacal super rhetoric advanced, in part, through of visual culture, I show that human rights photography relies on visual displays of particular (oppressed) raced and sexed bodies—to provoke fears, anxieties and resistances. The chapter traces the sensationalism around Mukhtar Mai, Aisha bibi and other human rights stories that became sensationalized, all of which relied on normative categories of the oppressed *cum* liberated brown women. Working from Inderpal Grewal's, Talal Asad's and Randall Williams's suggestions that human rights regimes misuse cultural narratives of the *other,* this chapter reveals that the human rights market masks the interstices of power over the *other* and how these stories come to enter the rights market are carried out through a number of erotic tropes.

The field of human rights, however, is not the only field of repre-

One. Vision as Violence

sentation that carries over from the Pakistani context to the U.S. context. Benazir Bhutto, who was heralded as global feminist icon and democratic célèbre in the U.S., is a key figure through whom we can deconstruct the power of a very specific sociopolitical fantasy around the feminine, racialized *other*. In the next chapter, "Is there a Queer Democracy? Or—Stop Looking Straight: Benazir Bhutto and the Hetero-Erotics of Democracy," I address the photographic representations of Bhutto and the consistent aestheticized framing of her to illustrate the way in which the images of Bhutto were able to provide meaning for the sustenance of American empire. In the midst of madly wrought representations of Pakistan as the "most dangerous place on earth," the figure of Benazir Bhutto emerged as both a stable and comfortable emblem of emancipated modernity and a visual opportunity to narrate empire through a multicultural heteronormative democracy. The mediums of public image making and visibility, in the case of Bhutto, are inextricably wedded to the conjoined mechanisms that systematically render Pakistani people uncivilized, uneducated, oppressed and backwards. The hyper–Western aestheticization of Bhutto contours deep structures of cultural exclusion and political delegitimization that fractures democracy, but also dresses colonial psychic wounds in amnesiac white contemporary fantasies.

In Chapter Five, "'Chicks with Sticks': Pleasure, Subversion and Insubordination in Female Political Subjectivity in Pakistan," I examine the 2007 globally publicized events of the Red Mosque in Islamabad, Pakistan, which brought front and center a fantastic fear of today's times: veiled Muslim women who engage in abrasive, anti–American, pro–Pakistan political action to their death. I assess the Lal Masjid photographic discourses to elucidate how media narrations and visualities function as mechanisms of power that discipline subjects across national borders, resolidifying notions of dangerous nations and paranoid citizenship. I argue that the U.S. heteronormative nation relies on, benefits from and eroticizes the (repressed) fe/male terrorists. I demonstrate how these women martyrs transgress and protect geopolitical borders and gender/sexual borders, in ways that are both disavowed and fetishized by the U.S. state. In interrogating the paranoid disciplining of these women through visual culture (as well as through brute force), I work towards a nuanced understanding of the political complexities these women raise for decolonial practice.

In the closing coda, I return to my title, to rethink notions of authenticity, trauma and radical politics. I raise the question of the erasure of radical potentiality and subjectivity of my three figures, and more broadly those subjects that that come to *be seen* as real in the forced environments of war, terrorism, national instability, and patriarchy. I look at the ways the central thread of trauma continues to be a persistent spectre in Pakistani women's narratives and what possibilities we open up and open to if we betray, rather than continue, this hegemonic tradition.

Through a brute calculus of racism and imperial geopolitics emerges an interest in the Pakistani feminine/feminist subject, her brown female body, the story of her oppression, and the question of her (as) nation. The public and personal texts produced for and by these women are implicated in a colonizing enterprise that *others* the Pakistani woman, a condition that ascertains, albeit with different valences and contexts, whether the *other* is perceived with dread or desire. I trace these sensational female visual figures of Pakistan, all of whom have been subject to patriarchal paranoid violence, to explore this crisis of desire and detestation of the feminine, racialized *other.* The localized stories and figures I re-narrate do not produce a fragmented mosaic of unconnected stories nor do they produce a master narrative of global women's oppression; rather they are deeply and intricately connected through the globalizing ideologies and structures that this project seeks to unravel.

Two

Paranoid Archives
Pakistan in the Field of Visuality, War and Empire

In September 2007, *National Geographic's* cover displayed a headshot of a brown-skinned, young Pakistani man, his light brown eyes, serious and sober, directly looking at the camera. His mouth is firm, his face, bearded. He is not smiling. The cover reads, "Islam's Fault Line: Pakistan." When the reader opens to the article, they see displayed on the first opening page, the face of a woman (**see fig. 2**): brown-skinned, mouth closed, head lowered, her hair and much of her face loosely covered by a blue chiffon *dupatta* through which we can make out a light profile of her nose decorated with a small, gold nose-ring, her lips unenhanced by makeup, her jaw line, while chiseled, seems resigned as it drops down. The woman's posture is lowered and her gaze cast downward. We cannot see her eyes. The picture gives off an aura of sadness and fatality. On one hand, we see this woman but cannot know her. On the other hand, she is made known to us even as she remains (fully) unseen. Fundamentally, she is invisible even as this photograph seeks to render her visible as contemporary global (oppressed) woman, as de facto Pakistan. One the opposite page, the article title, by Don Belt, reads, "Struggle for the Soul of Pakistan."

Truly, this photograph—nor the cover photo—tells the viewer anything about Pakistan, Pakistani women or men. She, specifically, could be a number of things. But her appearance on the cover of *National Geographic*,[1] a magazine widely critiqued for inviting "readers to look out at

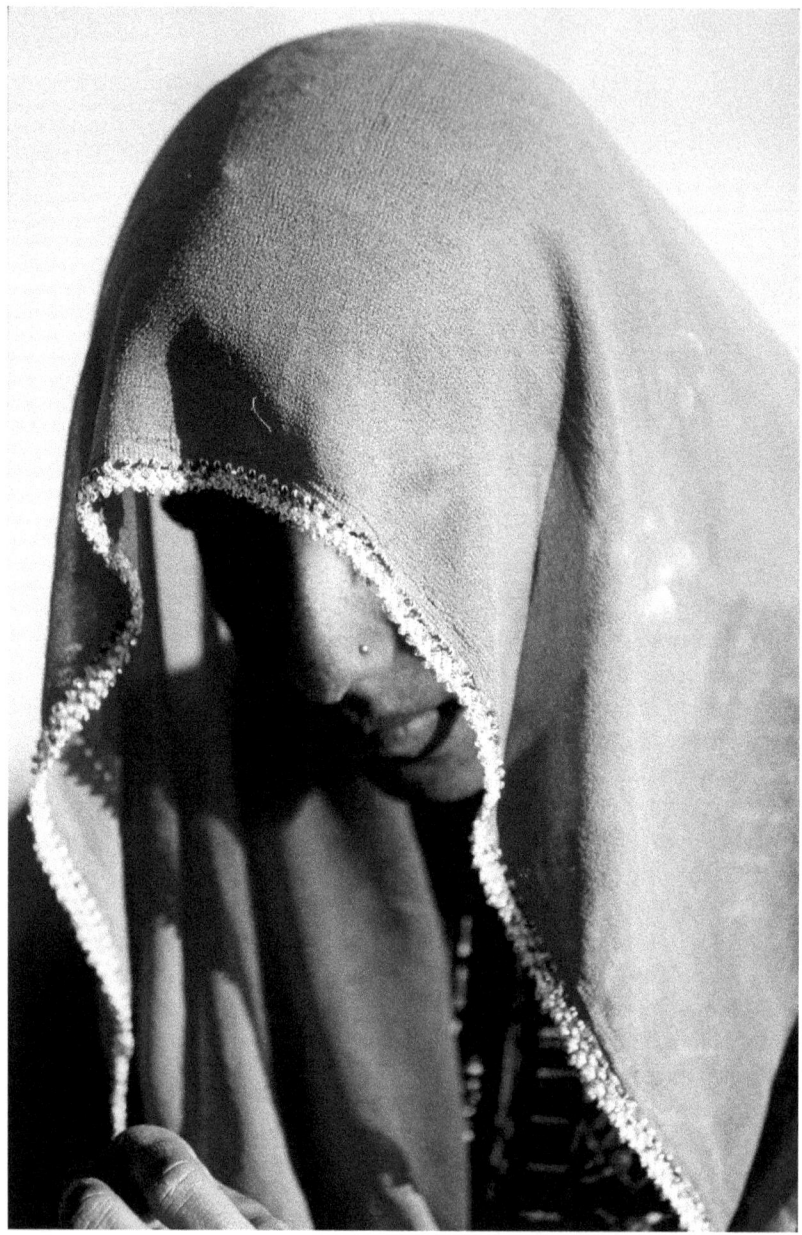

Figure 2. Multan, Pakistan, Koranic school in the city of Multan, Pakistan (*National Geographic*, September 2007. Photograph by Reza).

Two. Paranoid Archives

the rest of the world from the vantage point of the world's most powerful nation" (Lutz and Collins, 1993:7), the title of the cover story and the subtle affect-producing aesthetic posits both the photographed woman and the nation-state of Pakistan as imagined through a specific feminine, racialized corporeality. The photograph successfully evokes anxiety through a number of tropes—the downcast expression, the ethnicized aesthetic (i.e. nose-ring, hand-embroidered hair scarf, the plainness of the brown skin). The angle of the camera gives, perhaps intentionally, the viewer only half access to the woman's face, giving off the dual impression that she is a subject (of importance) yet, also seems to lack subjectivity. Every dimension of this photograph commands emotion, promising knowledge about the *other*.

Like the scene in *SATC2*, this photograph positions Pakistani/brown women and their bodies as a central site of American sociopolitical spectatorship. In part, the power of this woman's photograph is the way it resituates the contemporary colonial context as responsibly revitalizing the women subject, a subject otherwise dead by Pakistani culture; and in doing so, it authorizes itself as a crucial site of surveillance on the feminine, racialized *other*. *National Geographic*, insomuch as the image places the brown woman within context of understanding Pakistan's soul (or lack thereof) reenacts an old Orientalist fantasy of the mysterious character of the East and of the brown woman, simultaneously repulsive and tantalizing. It is this process of exposing the feminine, racialized *other*, sometimes literally denuding her (as in *SATC2*) that comes to allegorize U.S. masculinist power of possession. She, as metaphor for land, becomes available for Western penetration and knowledge. Combined, both image and words direct the audience toward some meanings (the soul of Pakistan is degenerative because of the status of women and the danger of Pakistani men) and away from others (the desperate realities of Pakistan generated, in large part, by U.S. intervention in the region, dated, at the least, to Cold War securitization). Indeed, it is striking that a man's unsmiling, serious face is used to underscore Pakistan as "Islam's fault line," while a women's half-hidden, lowered face is displayed to call attention to the soul of the nation. The space of visually telling the Pakistani wo/man's story has already been well prepared in ideological fantasizing.

The article in the *National Geographic*, itself a four-page spread, centers largely on the political and economic history of Pakistan, its processes of militarization, its relationship to India, and the growing seeds of Islamic resurgency. Only briefly does it engage with more civil dimensions of the Pakistan's trajectory, such as healthcare, education, and women's issues. The irony of the article relying on a stylized photograph to depict an oppressed woman *as* nation in order to engage in a discussion that only peripherally involves women's rights/roles in Pakistan is noteworthy. In their provocative book, *Reading National Geographic* (1993), Catherine Lutz and Jane Collins show how images emerging out of the global south, historically and contemporaneously, have largely been exotic, idealized, naturalized and sexualized. Arguing that *National Geographic* both produces and represents knowledge, Lutz and Collins underscore the erotic elements woven in the display of brown bodies for the white gaze insofar as the predominant reader of National Geographic is, more often than not, a white, middle-class, (straight) fe/male. In rendering Pakistan visible and sensational through the landscape of the female body, this *National Geographic* image, too, is interlaced with an eroticization of the brown female body. By honing in on the lowered face, the dominant gaze lays claim to the undeniable pleasures afforded to those who can *look* at iconic, Pakistani femininity.

For the American press, and its audience, it is axiomatic that photographs are a reliable source of knowledge on the *other* (Smith 1999; Barthes 1981; Tagg 1988; McClintock 1995). The visual coordinates that fix this woman as victim of Pakistan inevitably invokes *reality* in that it is perceived as adequately reflecting that which is outside itself; in this case, the *reality* of Pakistani women's lives. The photograph's power (and pleasure) lies in its successful ability to conceal its constructedness. The circuitous patterns of fetishistic disavowal of the (hegemonic) self vis-à-vis visual experience/fantasy of the *other* can be traced in the long history of colonial photography. Shawn Michelle Smith (1999), in a provocative exploration of American archival photography, argues that the self-defining mechanism of American photography has been its power to maintain middle-class white supremacy even as both whiteness and class appear invisible. This is because whiteness, Smith (1999) continues, secures its cultural power by seeming to do/be nothing at all, by being invisible. Historical photographs of early America are nonetheless racial documents in that they reinstate power even as they deny it. Frederic Jameson's (1981) argues that mass culture is neither entirely manipulative nor entirely authentic. In Jameson's view, images operate by arousing fantasies and desires within structures that diffuse them. Mass culture could not do its ideological work, if on some level, it did not utilize

Two. Paranoid Archives

utopian ideals. It could not manage desires and anxieties about social order if it did not deal in fears and fantasies that are recognizable. Hence, mass cultural imagery pleases the eye through the spectacle of particular bodies and violations of those bodies, both of which then seem to exist at a distance from the viewer.

In this regard, this photograph of Pakistan (through the landscape of the female body) operates, too, as a double bluff because even as it takes us in and acutely distances us. As visual image and global reality, this photograph assuages and arouses profound social and political anxieties and desires regarding white, middle-class privilege in an international class system. Invoking knowledge on what it takes to be a free subject, this photograph of Pakistan provides us with a position from which to say: "Yes, I am free." We are not her, but she can become one of us—the *other* folded into the U.S. embrace. We can congratulate ourselves on our perspicacity. The contours of this image interpellate the viewer into a specific subject position—culturally competent, empathetic Western viewer—an individual seduced by the image even as she is comfortably distanced from its reality.

This shot, like many of the photographs I will introduce in this book, functions as the prototypical "object-to-be-looked-at," inviting a fetishizing, voyeuristic gaze that simultaneously races and sexualizes its object. The utility of this deeply gendered, ethnicized and classed photograph of a Pakistani woman to represent the "struggle for Pakistan's soul," I argue, reveals a different economy of imperial desire and U.S. power that is reliant on the body schemata of brown women—bodies I name as *feminine, racialized others*.

A number of postcolonial thinkers, such as Franz Fanon (1967), Edward Said (1979), Gayatri Spivak (1987), and Albert Memmi (1965), have articulated a sense of the *other* at the very heart of history, culture and politics. In recent years, we've seen the revitalization of the imperial impulse to make visible the danger or deprivation of the Muslim *other*— an *other* imagined through sexuality, gender, race and nation (Puar, 2007; McClintock 2009; Abu-Lughod, 2003). Visual culture provides the logical step from this imagined sensibility to the actual production of the *other*, allowing the hegemonic gaze to both visualize and secure racial, national and gender difference (Mulvey 1977). The recent hyper-visibility of (Muslim) women has led to a proliferating field of questions on the political import of such visibility. As such, feminist postcolonial scholars have provided us with rigorous feminist models for understanding how empire and nation are articulated through women and their bodies, deconstructing the metonymic relation of race, gender, and sexuality to the formation of the nation-state and empire (Sangari 1999; Mohanty 2003; Alexander 2005).

The staging of American ethical superiority through the landscape of the oppressed brown female body (*National Geographic*), and hence, the U.S. (white) woman as already free (*SATC2*), rhetorically and literally, utilizes women's bodies and feminism as a visible and tangible site of global democratic reform (Sangari 1999). Oppressed citizenship (i.e. the trope of oppressed Muslim) is, then, articulated through its flipside—the absolute freedom of White American women—offered by white hands, the click of the camera, and acceptance of American visibility and sexualized/aestheticized liberty (as we see in *SATC2*).

The master narrative of the oppressed Muslim woman (and its many variants in France, Britain, and the United States) is constructed with a certain internal logic and presupposed relationship between visibility, representation and the female subject. The work of Chandra Mohanty (1991) has shown clearly how the discursive imposition of "western eyes," flattens the multiple experience of a vast number of women over a vast terrain. This process dates back to the onset of colonialism and the subsequent juggle of colonial to postcolonial to neocolonial temporalities (Scott 2007). Through this positioning of the Muslim woman, the liberal feminist consolidates her own position as free and liberated, in the process masking her own largely hopeless challenges to the neoliberal Western state in which she lives as inconsequential. At the same time, liberal feminist articulations of the Muslim woman help endorse Western military adventures in third world societies, a state that frequently ignores feminist organizing and demands for social change at home.

Visual images of (oppressed) Muslim women have come into a certain prominence now because of the dynamic force with which they speak broadly to gender and sexuality injustices, even as they are co-opted as symbols of national conflicts, nationalist projects, and national resistance movements in ways that often do not serve women's interests (Kandiyoti 1992; Kelley, Bayes and Hawkesworth 2001). A key example is the way the war in Afghanistan was strategically rationalized through both the language of feminism and the imaginaries of oppressed Muslim women's bodies (Ferre and Ali 2006, Eisenstein 2007, Butler 2004). But as we know, the U.S. doesn't only seduce its opponents through pleasure (of possible freedom). It is prepared to use devastating force.

Two. Paranoid Archives

As a postcolonial Muslim state in a direct dialectical relationship with the United States and the global war, Pakistan offers a particularly unique lens for us to understand how the contemporary proliferation of the woman subject is mired in a strange chasm between the univocality of global rhetoric such as democracy, the unadulterated but oft-mediated transit and utility of international visual culture and the polyvocality of local interpretations of femininity and feminism. Moving away from both the leftist tendency to see "Pakistan as the pilfered bottom to the Unites States imperial topping" (Roy 2008) or popular framings of Pakistan as a patriarchal, under-privileged nation-state that creates the conditions under which such subjects (of global intrigue) are constituted (Kristoff 2009), I posit Pakistan as (too often) ideologically signified and discursively organized vis-à-vis the racial and gendered structuring of the fe/male body and the woman subject.

There is little dispute that Pakistan's global visibility is largely catalyzed by the events of September 11, 2001. In November of 2010, ousted-Pakistani President Pervez Musharraf told *Newsweek*, "The world is watching Pakistan, and rightly so. It's a happening place." In fact, many scholars demonstrate the ways in which the events of September 11th both allowed the U.S. to be seen (in ways perhaps it had never been seen historically) and see others who were, up to that moment, largely invisible to the global eye (Mirzeoff 1998; Alexander 2005; Butler 2004). But, while 9/11 is a key descriptive hinge used to frame contemporary events of the war and its consequential burgeoning images, I want to work against any American exceptionalism in my reference to the events, though it is, obviously, an index of a certain kind of rupture for periodization, or as Inderpal Grewal (2005) notes, a fulfillment of earlier histories of Islamophobia, now transnationalized. In referring, then, to 9/11, I allude largely to a moment marked by the rise of imperial expansion, the policing, detention and deportation of immigrants, the construction of the foreign (brown) enemy, and the rise of Islamophobia, fundamentalist Christianity, the theocratic state and heterosexism, all of which are used to prop up the heated, and often violent, global dialectic between "third world" nationalism and notions of Western democracy and equity (Alexander 2005). The mediatization of events on 9/11 created new forms and techniques of Islamophobia and brought along intensified scrutiny of politicized forms of Islam. In this context gender, sexuality and race are enlisted in a variety of ways to legitimize and bolster Islamophobic discourses and practices. While Islamophobia is thought to have intensified since 9/11, such a presupposition problematically places the United States in the center of life across the planet. In the United States and in many other places across the globe, especially in Western Europe, there is surely an increase in Islamophobic profiling, criminalization, harassment, persecution, incarceration and disappearances. However, in many of these sites, including the United States, there is a long history of slower and more insidious Islamophobia formations in nearly all registers of life from dominant and popular culture (from opera and ballet to world fairs, cinema, music, etc.) to (official) governmental and juridical practices and discourses. The visual fields of Pakistan produced by global mediascapes need to be situated in wider geopolitics to understand how the woman question is now rearticulated through Muslim women's bodies and the fact that the proliferation of global Islamophobia is engendered by the war but also importantly predates 9/11.

Both the recent fetishization of Pakistan as "the most dangerous place on earth" and the U.S. neoliberal presumption/articulation of Pakistan as a failed state register an authority to visual cultural industries, through which we come to *see* corporealities of Pakistan and the wo/man subject. In 2008 Pakistan was named "the most dangerous place on earth," by both *Newsweek* (November 2008) and the *Economist* (January 2008). In 2007, Jon Moreau of *Newsweek*, clip elaborates the political concerns that dip images and narrations of Pakistan in U.S. paranoia.

> Today no other country on earth is arguably more dangerous than Pakistan. It has everything Osama bin Laden could ask for: political instability, a trusted network of radical Islamists, an abundance of angry young anti–Western recruits, secluded training areas, access to state-of-the-heart electronic technology, regular air service to the West and security services that don't always do what they're supposed to do. (Unlike in Iraq or Afghanistan, there also aren't thousands of American troops hunting down would-be terrorists.)

As the Moreau clip points out, Pakistan is rhetorically framed as an angry, armed and radically Islamic country either without democracy or with a false sense of it. Unlike Afghanistan and Iraq, Pakistan's war is seen as internally implosive with real possibilities of being externally explosive (to the West). These paranoid fears were only corroborated in April of 2011 with the discovery and assassination of Osama Bin Laden just outside Islamabad, the state's capital city, further substantiating conspiratorial panics and sharpening brutal force in the region.[2] For anyone who has even rudimentary knowledge of what has transpired in Pakistan over the last, say forty years, this image of Pakistan is ruthless in its omission (e.g., British colonial politics that led to the formation of Pakistan, U.S. practices during Cold War securitization, oscillating between militarizing Pakistani to abandoning the nation, among others). Indeed, Pakistan is a complicated site, both internally and with respect to its place in the world. Pakistan has and continues to experience both a reterritorialization of the homeland, through tumultuous acts of terror, political instability and ethnic conflict, as well as a simultaneous deterritorialization of the nation, through U.S. violence and dogmatic political demands as well as global social intervention (Khan 2007; Weiss 2003; Jamal 2005). Pakistan's exceptional position in the global war and the U.S.'s exceptional interest in Muslim wo/men have become the twin sites of paranoia and pleasure in the last decade.

Not surprisingly then, in order to tap into U.S paranoia and depict Pakistani danger, the October 2008 *Newsweek* utilized a provocative cover photograph that displayed a mass of angry, brown men in an unnamed protest, their arms raised and mouths open with smoke in the foreground (http://www.huffingtonpost.com/2007/12/28/newsweeks-prescient-pakis_n_78522.html). The paranoid obsessions of U.S. society which produce this image is stressed by the open mouths, raised arms, angry faces, the mixed images of anger, passion, emotional irrationality, all foregrounded by smoke. It is striking to note that the framing of Pakistan as "dangerous" relies on largely masculinist imagery, through brown male corporeality as aggressive, dirty, barbaric (*Newsweek*) or in masculinist abstraction, as the January 2008 issue of *The Economist* (http://www.economist.com/node/10430237) used a single hand grenade, painted green with the emblem of the Pakistani flag, standing in for a symbol of a dangerous masculine nation, with the text "The World's Most dangerous Place."

The language used by Moreau (2007) in the *Newsweek* article combined with the image appearing in a later *Newsweek (2008)* work together to construct an imaginative geography that dovetails with two claims of Pakistan's exceptionalism—its unique ability to support U.S. counterterrorist (counter-Islamic) efforts and its radical potential to sleep with the enemy Edward Said (1979) writes that Occidental masculinity relies on geopolitical fantasies of brown male violence, often Muslim men. Zygmunt Bauman (2005) argues that, in racism, one "exists before one acts," thus making one's qualification as an enemy "something one bears as a body." Such depictions of racialized Muslim masculinity have become the mainstay of a post–9/11 collective imagination, underscoring how constructions of the U.S. nation depend on particular understandings of both white domination (i.e. other nations as dangerous and barbaric) and heteronormativity (i.e. brown/Muslim men as hyper-heterosexual, herd-like and terrorizing). This is reified (in jest) by the *SATC2* scene, which demonstrates anxieties about the inevitability of brown men's violence and testifies to the entertainment value of this unfurling masculinity.

Juxtaposed to the *National Geographic* image, the contrast collides in a striking manner. It reifies the stereotype of oppressed, humble femininity against hyper-patriarchal, angry masculinity. Muslim men's hyper-masculinity becomes one of the reasons that Pakistani women are believed to be oppressed, and, as I will show in the next chapter, the subsequent liberation of Pakistani women is on the agenda of several groups. For the U.S., the project is control of Pakistani men and this becomes a method of rationalizing drone attacks on Pakistan (*they are violent, look how they treat their women and therefore deserve to be bombed*). The demonization of Muslim men and the consistent representation of them as unintelligible, or only intelligible as dangerous, is key to the successful visual portrayals of Muslim women as intelligible, hence savable, through human rights, democracy and war (Puar 2007; Battharchaya 2008).

Combined and parceled out, these photographs expose that the geopolitical and biopolitical investment in Pakistan in the aftermath of 9/11 and throughout this war is (often) signified through the visual traversal of wo/men's bodies.

In the spectacular visual field of post–9/11, Pakistan is constituted in the imagination of the politically powerful as the *id* of the world. Academy Award winning film, *Zero Dark Thirty* (2013, Katherine Bigelow), which self-presents, however dubious, as a documentary is set almost completely in the back alleys of Pakistan (ironically, many parts of the film were filmed in Mani Majra, India—a small town next Chandigarh, where local residents protested that Indian land was being used to represent Pakistan). *Zero Dark Thirty* depicts the CIA's hunt for Osama Bin Laden and his eventual capture/assassination just outside Islamabad, Pakistan's capitol city. Nominated for a number of awards and netting approving nods from ten critics association including New York Film Critics Circle and National Board of Review, the film is the ultimate self-congratulations, which Slavoj Žižek (2013) wittingly calls, "Hollywood's gift to American power." *Zero Dark Thirty* further authenticates U.S.

paranoia and Pakistani danger by relying on the ideological portrayals of Western superiority using the familiar tropes of the quintessential (white) American liberal feminist woman determined to find and kill the bad buys, treacherous Muslim men, and the invisibility (literally) of brown/Muslim women. Bigelow's film, which arguably catalyzed her to even more fame than her academy award for *The Hurt Locker*, glorifies (white) female determination and persistence in a world dominated by (white) men, where Pakistan and its fe/male subjects are worthy only of momentary sentimentality (not dissimilar to *SATC2*). *Zero Dark Thirty* and *SATC2*, however strikingly different forms of entertainment, both mobilize the narrative spectacle of Muslim/brown subjects and the perfected feminism of the white west, without taking responsibility for the meaning and weight of it images. The recent interface of the global visual industry and these cinematic forms of faux-feminist imperatives reveals what Angela McRobbie (2009:5) calls, "an aggressive individualism, by a hedonistic female phallicism." I would add, here, that these forms of female phallicism are strategically and predominantly shaped by both whiteness and imperialism. The cinematic moment in *SATC2* and the film *Zero Dark Thirty* demonstrate that even something as incidental as mainstream entertainment codifies forms of domination masked as simultaneous (Muslim) documentation and (white) entertainment.

The increasing prolific transit between the ideology of human rights and/or democracy and the visual cultural industry marks the ascendency of these visual subjectivities as the privileged frame for Pakistan, and more broadly, Muslim *nation-state*s and The Muslim Woman. However, colonial and neocolonial forms of knowledge are inextricably folded into these contemporary visualities and stories of Pakistani wo/men, both further punctuated by the forces of transnational networks and processes (Appadurai 1996). The ideological implications of these photographic and cinematic narrations replicate narrow racial, class, sexual, gender and national ideologies, which then, facilitates political paranoia while authorizing the white racial state's ethical superiority.

Pleasure and Paranoia: Empire's Pakistan

A central concern of this book is to analyze how the transnational proliferation of photographs of brown/Muslim wo/men is largely justified through a narrative discourse of paranoia and pleasure, where both revolve around particular bodies and subjects, aesthetics and freedoms (Foucault 1977; Williams 2010). Like the moment in *SATC2*, the sensational images discussed in this chapter demonstrate that displays of brown bodies are not merely ideological distortions convenient to an emergent global political order, but densely crafted visual fields that organize and produce Pakistan wo/men as political and pleasurable reality (McClintock 1995). This desire to render Pakistan transparent through the landscape of the fe/male subject requires an examination of the politics of representation with the domain of desire, power, and subjectivity.

Taking a close look at Ann McClintock's (2009, 53) work around Empire, she argues that the U.S. state has entered the domain of paranoia, "for it is only in paranoia that one finds simultaneously both deliriums of pleasure for the *other* and forebodings of the perpetual threatening *other*." McClintock conceptualization of paranoia as "a way of seeing and being attentive to contradictions within power, a way of making visible the contradictory flashpoints of violence that the state tries to conceal" (McClintock 2009, 53), shifts paranoia from a primary structure or characteristic of U.S. imperialism, to an unstable tension that shapes the ways in which the U.S. imagines and articulates nativized and racialized *others*. In naming the U.S. a paranoid empire, McClintock does not suggest that the U.S. alone has entered a domain of paranoia. Clearly, traces of paranoia towards/against the other can be traced in France, Italy among other Western countries. I, however, do argue that in the U.S., this paranoia has distinct visual dimensions that are unique to the media–driven culture of the U.S.

This paranoia, in the context of the war on terror, is strikingly productive even as it aggrandizes racialized violence. This is most notably exemplified by the 2003 globally discoursed tortures, where political torture manifested as erotic via *seen* acts of S&M, hooding, forced sodomy, public sex. Islamophobia and Orientalism guided the manipulation and deployment of queer sexualities in Abu Ghraib. Abu Ghraib perfectly (and tragically) elucidates the ways (Muslim) bodies become sites through which dominion is enacted, on sexual lines through visual culture. The storm of controversy around the Abu-Ghraib photographs brought an acute awareness to the semiotic and material racializations and sexualizations of Muslims in the war on terror. As McClintock (2009) notes, the power to *see* the *other* (in this case, naked and sexed) became equated with the power to know and to dominate.

Emerging discourses on U.S. exceptionalism since 9/11 have deeply

Two. Paranoid Archives

sexual and paranoid dimensions (Puar 2007; McClintock 2009; Faludi 2006). Jasbir Puar (2007), in her groundbreaking monograph *Terrorists Assemblages*, points to both these dimensions as she names the U.S. a heteronormative state. Puar (2007) argues that both heteronormativity and homonationalism are at play in U.S. nation-state building—the state as heteronormative and homonationalist, whereby the latter utilizes model gay citizens to corroborate the ethical superiority of the white racial state, through specific multicultural identities (i.e. white middle-class gay men and/or white feminist women) just as it maintains the pathology of racial *others* that don't fit this emerging consumer/legislative model (i.e. dangerous Muslim men). Pointing to the 9/11 industry machine, Puar makes it is patently clear that LGBT liberation also works to distract attention from the increasing racialization of Muslim bodies, which lends itself to various forms of intense criminalization of Muslims. Puar (2007) underscores how the Muslim *other* is constructed as a productive foil to the liberated U.S. citizen and to liberatory U.S. practices, where citizenship and citizen practices, i.e., representation, work as reflective surfaces that allow empire to avoid seeing itself. Both scholars propose a profound challenge to the politics and pleasures of visibility, visuality and violence.

Within the changing modes of visibility and surveillance that emerge under globalization, being a *seen* subject enables securitizing technologies, such as in the recent 2011 French debates around the veil (see, e.g., Joan Scott, *Politics of the Veil*), the Abu Ghraib scandal and/or as I will demonstrate in the 2007 Lal Masjid conflict, even as these same technologies tap into a liberal ethos of individual empowerment. In this way, representations which grant visibility to otherwise unseen subjects function as a key mechanism for solidifying empire, albeit in ways that is neither always consistent nor neat. We have learned from Michel Foucault (1978) that increasing visibility leads to power located on increasingly individualized and corporeal levels, a major strategy of which is surveillance. Following Jasbir Puar (2007), I see sexuality and the surveillance of Pakistani women's bodies in the wake of 9/11 as inseparably linked in that "discourses of counterterrorism are intrinsically gendered, raced, and sexualized and that they illuminate the production of imbricated normative patriot and terrorist corporealities that cohere against and through each other" (p. xxiv). I propose that these photographs of Pakistan and Pakistani women function neither as a liberal structure of modernity nor as just a problematic subject position, but as an assemblage of neoliberal economics, contemporary biopolitics and the governing of Muslim/brown citizens along lines of on sex, race, gender and nation.

Pushing this further, Abu Ghraib (as well as *SATC2* and the *National Geographic* photograph) disturbingly demonstrated that alongside this production of *seen* bodies, meanings of the body are partly produced in a semiotically infused physical exchange of erotic energy between object-looked-upon and the adoring/disgusted gaze (Rose 2007; Zita 1998; Jones 2003). The disciplinary opportunity in being seen is not wholly separate from the erotic underbelly that allows for a *jousiance*[3] in seeing the *other*. I deliberately invoke the Lacanian (1992) notion of *jouissance*, where *jouissance* is distinct from pleasure insofar as pleasure obeys the laws and limits of enjoyment and *jouissance* transgresses the laws of enjoyment. Jouissance goes beyond the pleasure principle and into a kind of troubling, excessive pleasure that includes elements of transgression, sexuality and suffering

The Lacanian concept of *jouissance* has a sexual connotation embedded with both raw pleasure and displeasure, tied perhaps to another key psychoanalytic concept—fetish. Fetish, here, is not simply really liking or desiring something. The key point of fetish is that it displaces and alleviates anxieties about the radical/primitive/violent *other*, transferring powerful or taboo energies from that which can't be looked at or apprehended directly into something that can (Mulvey 1977). Hence, my critique of the pleasure interwoven in liberal and visual discourses, such as human rights and democracy, is not unfamiliar. It is a recognition that a banal feature of advanced capitalistic societies is the desire to consume. However, in firmly situating pleasure within the photographic fields of Pakistan, I push this recognition from a banal feature to a primary quality of the politico-cultural discourse.

I remind the reader that these next few chapters requires a reading that keeps taut the tension between the ideological, disciplinary and liberatory potential of these visual subjectivities. Examining these next three fields of Pakistani women's photographs is an effort to carefully delineate the masked problematic of the erotic gaze woven into the three axes of human rights, democracy, and the global war. To bring to scrutiny the authority of these visual stories is a task that requires reading visual practices and their rhetorical narratives as arising out of Empire's unfolding axes of war, democracy and human rights, and disturbing these habits of visually thinking about Pakistan, the woman subject, and feminist labor.

Three

Fetish, Fantasy and Freedom
Brown Women's Bodies as Subject of/to Human Rights

> *Something becomes real—to those who are elsewhere....*
> —Susan Sontag, 2004, 21

This chapter pivots off three gendered and racialized human rights stories that capture the relationship between human rights and its transnational transit in and through visual culture. The central imperative I take up is a deconstruction of the relationship between human rights and visual culture, where the latter is lionized as a piece de resistance in a putative race-neutral rights market. I frame human rights as a global ethic lauded as counterhegemonic but utilized in the service of hegemonic, imperial expansion (Williams 2010). I focus on human rights regimes as manifested in a post–September 11, 2001, visual culture—a popularized, powerful and transnationalized system of knowledge production on the racial *other* (Williams 2010; Grewal 2005).

As a megalomaniacal super rhetoric advanced, in part, through of visual culture, this chapter demonstrates that human rights photography relies on visual displays of particular (oppressed) raced and sexed bodies to provoke fears, anxieties and resistances. I begin by examining the visual and discursive texts surrounding—three significant visual moments in contemporary human rights discourses in the U.S after 9/11—2004 Pakistani gang rape victim Mukhtar Mai, the 2010 International Women's Day film, entitled *Half the Sky*, and *Time* Magazine's (August 2010) controversial photograph of Bibi Aisha. I consider the structure of these visual narrations and the modes of (un)intelligibility they move forward. I will show how the feminine, racialized body gets deployed as a metaphor for the restoration of freedom and functions as a key link in modern projects of bodily autonomy, visual objectification, and privileged subjectification. By interrogating the discursive chain of visual events that turned these women's lives into a story of American-style heroics, I work against the visible and cognizant field of sight that registers them as *real* oppressed women and interprets radical freedom as an accomplishment of developmental discourses. A close reading of these visual subjects reveal that such representations are coded with racialized eroticism, elucidating both complex productive fantasies and the striking interface of paranoia, power and pleasure.

Human Rights in a Field of Power

In the last decade, the brown female *other* has become increasingly drawn into racial and eugenics discourse, in ways that have placed her at the heart of imperialist, paranoid politics. Much of this discourse has relied on a collective visual imagination of her as the oppressed *other*. This idea of a common collective consciousness of the nation (around the *other*) is not a free-floating signifier: it is grounded in relations of domination and subordination. The way the white racial state, and its varying apparatuses, here the media, promotes a collectivity reinforces particular notions and practices of representation, storytelling and more broadly, discourse. These visual and narrative representations are simultaneously descriptive and moral, where moral projects are ultimately projects of normalizing, rendering natural and obvious prescriptions of the *other*. Here, then, the link between looking and authority is cemented.

Inderpal Grewal (2005) has shown that, since 9/11, an ethos of Americanism as a collective conscious has burgeoned as a cultural ethic and sensibility, both within and outside the borders of America. This sensibility has a palpable public presence, manifest in the vast proliferation of inter/national rhetoric, institutionally upheld ideologies and, most importantly, in marked displays of American-ness and the *other*. In this way, the explosive growth of photographs of varying Muslim nations in the last decades, including Pakistan, is perhaps the crucial geo-cultural event of our times. The most contemporary case of human rights in Pakistan is Malala Yousafzai, the 14-year-old girl who was shot in the head by members of the Taliban on October 9, 2012, for her vocal advocacy of girls' education. She is now the "world-famous survivor" of a Taliban assassination attempt, an activist for girls' education and winner of the Nobel Peace Prize in 2014. Malala's book, *I am Malala*, written by British journalist Christina Lamb was released in 2013. While this chapter focuses on the sensationalized case of Mukhtar Mai (2004), Malala's more recent romanticized globalized popularity as a Pakistani women's rights activists (at the tender age of 11, which is when *New York Times* journalist, Adam Ellick, met and wrote an article introducing her and plight of girl's education in Swat, Pakistan) demonstrates that U.S. stories of Pakistani danger and oppression continue to unfold through the axis of racialized and gendered surveillance and suspicion. I will return to Malala at the end of this chapter.

As visual subject par intrigue, the feminine, racialized *other* index the current socio-cultural and political configuration that relies on what Spivak (1988, 297) calls, the "subject-deprivation of the brown female." The incessant dependence on visualizing the *other* as deprived supports the neoliberal imagination that locates notions of self and freedom in an agentic, autonomous and rational subject, with access to market freedoms, where human and market freedoms emphatically unify. The *SATC2* scene with which this book opens most certainly exemplifies this amalgamation between women and market freedoms. Like *SATC2*'s reliance on the visual performance of Muslim women meeting emancipation through the act of disrobing, human rights discourses heavily relies on visual displays of oppressed, feminine, racialized bodies, through which the viewer comes to sympathize with the *other*, and develop a phantasmic relation to this *other* as erotic, exotic, and in dire need of (white) saviors (even when they are saving themselves).

Randal William (2010) interrogates this burgeoning fascination with the human rights of racial *others* and how media and cinematic narrations of these black/brown subjects produces the U.S. American subject as global citizen *par excellence*. Through an analysis of the renowned film, *Hotel Rwanda*, Williams (2010, 35) writes that because the (neo)colonial context is inherently dehumanizing and inegalitarian, and relies on specific displays of brown and black bodies, it deprives both human rights discourse and the subjects to which they speak, of freedom or even humanity. Williams (2010) argues that the power of human rights lies in obscuring the relationship between imperial violence, international law, and U.S. benevolence. Contemporary formations of human rights have hegemonic contours that merge human rights and imperialism in a symbiotic relationship (Williams 2010; Hunt 2007; Puar 2007; McClintock 2009). We see this in both *National Geographic's* utility of a woman's body to depict the soulless nation of Pakistan and in *SATC2's* visual depiction of dangerous brown men and secretively coutured veiled women.

Amira Jarmakani's (2008) work on U.S. representations of Arab womanhood punctuates this point. Using the case of the famous Afghan girl,[1] whose iconic image came to symbolize the plight of Afghanistan and was rediscovered after 9/11, this time in full *niqab*, Jarmakani elucidates how representations of Muslim women unfasten women's stories/realities from their complex conditions and erect them as signifiers of dominant ideologies of liberal humanism, U.S. exceptionalism, and third world barbarisms. Jarmakani (2008) traces U.S. representations of Arab woman, ranging from the belly dancer to the veiled oppressed woman, and argues that rather than revealing something about Arab and Muslim cultures, the images bespeak that peculiarly patriarchal logic of U.S. militarism in the war on terror. Both these authors show that visual manifestations of human rights run the risk of flattening women's experience into the all too seductive binary of *us* and *them*, narrating brown/Muslim women's bodies in ways that ultimately serves to justify military interventions (Grewal 2005; Esteva and Prakash 1998). Malala's Yousafzai attempted assassination by the Taliban confirmed and rationalized the need for, what is often called, the secret drone war in Pakistan. The allure of Malala's tragedy now, like previously Mukhtar Mai's, is deeply connected to the geopolitical and biopolitical complexities of the global war.

Hence, women's rights as human rights operate within a broader discursive formation shaped U.S. exceptionalism, war and paranoia. At a theoretical level, we have learned from the labors of postcolonial thought that, too often, gender justice and radical women's rights work has been saturated by human rights rhetoric, developmental concerns of/for women in the global south, and women's NGO movements (Grewal 2006), or what Lila Abu-Lughod (2010) calls, "the NGO-ization of feminism." Adding to this, Jacqui Alexander (2005) argues, orientalism assumed a certain form when it traveled within women's studies, producing its own variant of alterity in the figure of the non–Western, tradition-bound woman. The analytical move in Western feminism that ultimately produced the persecuted woman subject utilizes a universal woman, avoiding the histories of genocide, American/Western domination and neoliberal exploitation of these very same subjects. For the most part, this elision has been established and promulgated by the narrative of violence against women, in which protectionist arguments become the primary narrative.

Protectionists' arguments appear to be inherent in any women's issues, in that any discussion on gender-based oppression may generate victim *cum* savior narratives. They are not altogether easy to avoid, nor are they necessarily insincere. However, there are multifarious relations of domination and subordination that circulate within the term "protection," in ways that defer, mask or sugarcoat their meaning. Pathak and Rajan (in Butler and Scott 1992, 263) argue that discourses of protection directed at Muslim women serve to camouflage power politics. In their analysis, Pathak and Rajan (1992, 263) elucidate how, within the ideological parameters of protection, "an alliance is formed between protector and protected against a common opponent from whom danger is perceived and protection offered and sought and this alliance tends to efface the will to power exercised by the protector."

Certain international configurations of women's-rights-as-human-rights projects based in the west are critiqued for imposing Western notions of the self, of the human, of rights on postcolonial societies in modes that collude with Western governments or operationalize the colonial savior narrative (Spivak 2000; Mahmoud 2005; Al-Ali 1999). The post–9/11 period has in fact marked a systematic codification of this move to establish international humanitarian norms for civilian protection, where the civilians in need are de facto seen as brown (Muslim) women, or increasingly gay Muslims. For these scholars, women's-rights-as-human-rights represents the apotheosis of what has been called the dehistoricized and deterritorialized mapping of others (Abu Lughod 2010, Mahmoud 2005; Grewal 2005; Spivak 2000). Women's-rights-as-human-rights is an offshoot of human rights regimes, by which we see the networks of knowledge, representation and power that inserted these discourses into geopolitics. Such theorizations necessitate a broader understanding of the ways women's right gets visually catalogued on and around the feminine, racialized *other*—a woman who is often, but not always a Pakistani woman. How, then, are the bodies of Pakistani women serving broader political purposes?

Mukhtar Mai as Metaphor and Reality of/for Pakistan

The March 2005 cover of the *New York Times* magazine showcases a woman—brown skin, dark eyes, head bowed, gaze lowered, head covered loosely, sublime, humbled and tragic (**see fig. 3**). The photograph is mostly a headshot. The viewer is privy to her drooping shoulders, a deliberately lowered posture implying that she is humbled, shamed, broken. Her hair is covered loosely with a black headscarf, *dupatta*, with wisps of black hair coming through. A tear gathers at the corner of one eye. She

Figure 3. Mukhtar Mai, a victim of gang rape, sheds tears after a court's decision in Multan, Pakistan, on March 3, 2005 (AP Photo/Khalid Tanveer).

Three. Fetish, Fantasy and Freedom

is not looking at the camera. The absence of her direct gaze suggests she is a woman in fear, in distress. Her trauma is etched on her face; the brutality of her circumstance comes through. A mere look at this image invokes a tremendous emotional reaction. We are made to wonder. We sympathize. We empathize. We grieve.

This photograph is of Mukhtar Mai—a 30-year-old Pakistani woman from Meerwala, Pakistan, who was publicly gang raped and paraded naked before hundreds of onlookers in her village as a form of honor revenge. In many cases, women who have been humiliated by such public sexual violence have or have been expected to commit suicide after such an event. Mai, however, decided to press charges, and took her case to court. Mai's case was first brought to the judicial eye by a male Muslim cleric, picked up by the Human Rights Commission of Pakistan (HRCP), and then fought by Asma Jahangir,[2] well-known Pakistani women's rights activist. Her rapists were arrested and charged.

At that time, Mai won. In 2004, six men involved in her rape were sentenced to death and the government awarded her compensation, approximately 43,800 Rupees (U.S. $7,300). However, the convictions were appealed and the Lahore High Court overturned five of the six convictions. Mai, again, appealed to the Supreme Court in 2005, but in April of 2011, the court rejected her appeal. According to Nicholas Kristoff (2009), a well-known writer for the *New York Times* and co-author of *Half The Sky: Turning Oppression Into Opportunity*, Mukhtar Mai, her friends, colleagues and their families continue to be at great risk from violence by local feudal lords, and/or the government of Pakistan. Mai remained in her village and has used the money to open a school for girls in their village, the Mukhtar Mai Women's Welfare Organization, and, in fact, tried to enroll her rapists' daughters in her school. The *Mukhtar Mai School for Girls* is in plain sight from the house where the four men raped her. She has also opened two other schools for girls, a crisis center for abused women, and a clinic offering free legal help. By no means a small feat, Mai and her work crucially mark the feminist culture and oppositional energy that emerges from such oppressive circumstances (even as she doesn't name it feminism).

Mai's case gained international attention in 2005, when then-president General Pervez Musharraf placed restrictions on her movement, claiming that her story could potentially hurt the international image of Pakistan. At that time, Asma Jahangir on *CBC*, Kristoff in the *New York Times*, and others in *TimeAsia* and *BBC*, all said that the

Will the Real Pakistani Woman Please Stand Up?

Musharraf administration had confiscated Mai's passport and prohibited her access to an American visa. That same year, 2005, *Glamour* Magazine named her "Woman of the Year." After much battling and with the help of Jahangir, Mai traveled to New York, her first trip out of Pakistan, to receive *Glamour* magazine's "Woman of the Year" award in the company of Hollywood stars such as Catherine Zeta Jones and Goldie Hawn. According to Cindi Leive (2005), Glamour's editor-in-chief, in choosing this awardee, *Glamour* looks for "strength ... persistence... a woman of the year is someone who believes that women can do whatever they set their mind to, and Mukhtar illustrates those qualities better than anybody. This is a story that's going to shock everyone who hears it."

In April 2007, Mukhtar Mai won the North-South Prize from the Council of Europe. Mai's story has been retold in the 2006 documentary *Land, Gold and Women* and in her autobiography, *In the Name of Honor: A Memoir* (2007). According to the *New York Times* (Kristoff 2009), Her autobiography is the No. 3 best seller in France, movies are being made about her, and she has been praised by dignitaries like Laura Bush and the French foreign minister. *Bitch* magazine, a well-known American feminist magazine, released a statement in February of 2009 that Mai's story will be the subject of an upcoming American feature film. According to a *BBC* profile article (2011), Mai's attack became the most infamous women's rights case in Pakistan for years.

Mukhtar Mai's story no doubt induces a social and cultural vertigo. Within Mai's story, Pakistan becomes the locus of the paranoid colonial and liberal gaze, and the U.S. emerges as a state of/for women's security and public empowerment. Here, we see the link between biopolitics and geopolitics in that security and care are cast as impossible in Pakistan because of the inherent violence attributed to its men. But through the American spotlight, security, safety and humanitarianism become possible. The *real* Pakistani woman gets legitimated in her humanitarian mission by virtue of a (non)fictionalized representation. Mai's story reinvigorates the 1970s feminist Orientalist scholarship[3] that defined Muslim women as passive others bereft of the enlightened consciousness possessed by their Western sisters, however, with a neoliberal twist. Mai, as a desirable subject of these neoliberal/neocolonial times, departs from this Orientalist fantasy and becomes, instead, a story of the disparaged Pakistani women who reaps justice (through the market) against all odds.

Fig. 3 of Mukhtar Mai is the most widely circulated image of her, first taken by the Associated Press, but reprinted over and over again by

Three. Fetish, Fantasy and Freedom

varying international presses, *New York Times, BBC, CBC*, as well as in a plethora of human rights, NGO and civil society websites such as Human Rights Commission of Pakistan (hrcp.org). This photograph incites the symbolic power of visual experience in the making of the feminine, racialized *other*. The reprinting of this image in presses around the Western world speaks volumes about the tremendous symbolic and discursive weight attached to racialized, female bodies and practices. As a largely unfinished, precarious but deeply redeeming visual story emerging under the umbrella of human rights, Mai's visual narrative becomes an exploratory analogy for the proverbial woman question. Through a particular coordination of her body, posture, and gaze, Mai is read as the *real* Pakistani woman.

By italicizing *real* I invoke the Lacanian (1992) sense of term, where the notion of the *real* is the state of nature from which we have been forever severed by our entrance into language. Hence, there is no real, or as Lacan states "the real is impossible" (Lacan in Žižek, 2008, 23). What we call "reality," Lacan tells us, is articulated through signification (the symbolic) and the characteristic patterns of images (the imaginary). This imaginary seeks to domesticate the symbolic through the imposition of fantasy, *joussaince* and ideology. Still, the *real* continues to exert its influence, to be something we constantly desire to see or express. The *real* is constituted in the interstitial spaces between images and ideologies, in constant tension with the symbols that try to capture it. This photograph, along with other visual human rights subjects in the Muslim world, is situated within this very idea of a transnational imaginary and the national symbolic, the (American) fantasy and *joussaince* of her *real* (Pakistani) story.

Looking at **fig. 3**, the image employs a number of visual devices to portray the *reality* of female oppression. Her head is bowed, her gaze lowered, her hair covered. Her headscarf is black with a slim multicolored slim embroidery along the border, framing her face in way that suggests sexual modesty, humility and national authenticity. Her eyes are dark and teary. She is mesmerizing, indeed arresting, in spite of her brutalization. It seems the camera has caught her unprepared, engrossed. She is almost folded into herself. She has been photographed in what seems her most natural state. The effect of this image is that Mai's tragedy, her "self" as a figure of global importance, has been made *known*. She exists outside of the West, made visible by the West, for the Westerner's view. And in being privy to her story, we become privy to a brutally gendered Pakistan. In capturing her essence, the viewer comes to know her. She is nature. We are culture, interpreting her.

Susan Sontag (1973) tells us that, "photographs really are experience captured, and the camera is the ideal arm of consciousness in its acquisitive mood. To photograph is to appropriate the thing photographed. It means putting oneself into a certain relation to the world that feels like knowledge—and, therefore, like power." The literal content of the image—Mai, her head scarf, her facial expression, her posture—works with the text of her story to invoke the tragedy of grand human suffering, woman's pains, emotional excess and emphatic conflicts that organize reality for women in the global south. As Rose (2007:138) states, "pictorial images perform a vital cognitive function in linking the ideological and the observable, materializing the ideology and fetishizing the object, instructing the mind through the education of the eyes." Each dimension of Mai's corporeal visual objectification is part of a system of perception that uses the female body to systematically map in/visible national and cultural characteristics. In rendering Mai visible and sensational, the image idealizes (even eroticizes) the oppressed female form. The posture of Mai's body provides a fluency in Pakistani women's grievances. It produces (invents) feelings of loss, despair, and a certain thoughtfulness on the role of women in (Pakistani) society. Her image points out and notifies, it makes us understand something and it imposes on us. As Sontag (2003:67) says, "the photograph has the deeper bite."

The visual regime that captured Mai took shape around the problem of saving Pakistani women. This photograph is an important indictment of Pakistan, a state visualized as organized by oppressive gender and sexual stratification rather than egalitarianism. Her tragedy is consumed as a spectacle from a point of privileged invisibility, a spectacle that relies on conceiving of culture in visual terms—"clearly bounded," "oppressed," "sexual savaged/s"—all of which are read through the female body. The photograph of Mai masks the state of gendered vulnerability in the U.S. and allows the Western women participate in the illusion that they are free and safe. Mai's hyper-symbolization as victim *cum* rights advocate (quite similar to the role Malala Yousafzai now stars in) engenders the idea that freedom and America are virtually interchangeable.

Mai's visual story contributes to dominant American liberal ideologies insofar as they produce and effectively sustain the American woman as transcendent subject and the Pakistani woman as immanent object. Within this dominant grid of intelligibility, freedom comes to exist within

Three. Fetish, Fantasy and Freedom

the individuals' ability to move from the state of in-itself to a state for-itself, where she acts and lives in a way that moves her from immanence to transcendence. In today's geopoliticized field of subjectivities, there is a notable trend in neoliberal, democratic institutions to celebrate this triumphant movement from immanent object of patriarchy to transcendental subject of the modern world (Grewal 2006; Esteva and Prakash 1998). In marking Mai as the *other*, the media simultaneously offer her a way to bypass marginality through the definitive strategy of visibility and voice, tropes strategically embodied by subject pour-soi.

Stuart Hall (1997) pushes us to pay close attention to the cultural processes by which the visible differences of appearance come to stand for natural properties of human beings. In **fig. 3**, the artificial auratic projection is intended to manipulate the subjective gaze for ideological/political purposes. This photograph of Mai is not a transparent window but rather an optic through which the hegemonic gaze can interpret her world. So the image(s) of Mai become the world of Pakistan. As a result, Pakistan is simultaneously incited and silenced, referenced and ungraspable. As the sublime in a field of geopolitical wars and nationalisms, Mai most effectively stands as witness to an encounter that is mostly unrepresentable—colonists' imagination of the *other*. The proliferation of Mai's image can be attributed to the vitality of a modernity that links the conquests of postcolonial photography to the victories of emancipation. As an evocative emotional visuality, the story of Mai cripples all complexities of the Pakistan-American geopolitical nexus; thereby serving as evidence for the prosecution of "foreign" nationalist patriarchy.

For example, in 2005, then-President Musharraf was accused of repossessing Mai's passport and keeping her from traveling to the U.S. where she had been invited to speak by Condoleezza Rice and *Glamour* Magazine, among others. According to Kristoff and WuDunn, in *Half the Sky*, Musharraf wanted "Pakistan to be known for its sizzling economy and not notorious for barbaric rapes" (2009:72). Musharraf was concerned with Mai's story going global as potentially "airing Pakistan's dirty laundry" and damaging the already tenuous position Pakistan held with America in the global war (Kristoff 2007). It can, of course, be argued that Musharraf, not unproblematically nor wholly inaccurately, recognized that Mai's entrance onto American soil was really an invitation into American living rooms, indeed into what Jose Munoz (1999:4) calls "suburban spectatorship," where her oppressed *cum* liberated body could be celebrated. In a *BBC* (2005) article, Mukhtar Mai stated, "But I feel the government is very suspicious of me. I wonder why? Maybe they feel had I gone to the U.S., I would have talked against Pakistan. Little do they know that had anyone dared say a word against my country I would have shut that person up there and then."[4] While Mai's statement works against the narrative of her rape being used as evidence of Pakistani barbarism (which indeed it was), it does so by indeed by rendering intelligible nationalist discourses. However, within hegemonic configurations of the Pakistani nation-state as questionable and U.S. visibility as unquestionable, Mai's statement takes on interesting dimensions.

While both dominant state and (inter)nationalist frameworks attempted to inculcate Mai into the domestic (and domesticated) human rights subject, Mai remained ambivalent and sometimes, even impossible. For example, in Mai's live *CBS* interview during her visit to the U.S, she was repeatedly asked, so what it is like to be gang raped? Mai indignantly replied: "I don't really want to talk about that." Kristoff (2009:73), the biggest advocate of her American visibility, noted that "Mukhtar had a disastrous live interview on the *CBS* morning news in which she was asked about it (the rape)." And when she refused to answer, Kristoff said, "there was an awkward silence." This was just one among many American interviews.

When Foucault (1978:59) said, "Western man has become a confessing animal," he points to the quintessential Western desire to confess, or hear to *others* confess—a confession which operates as the main ritual for the production of truth and plays a role in all realms of life, from forms of justice to states of victimhood. In this regard, personal narrative, as a cultural enterprise, has become so important that it functions as a commodity spectacle, where an individual's story becomes of great significance for public consumption and discourse. Mai was expected to confess her victim status, where confession is articulated as the price for freedom. The question, "what was it like" crystallizes the ways in which nationalism and empire are, yes, predicated on the notion of women's bodies as communal property (Boehmer 2000) but is also invested in these women's explicitly confessional stories.

Like Fanon's (1965) Antillean spectator who suddenly finds himself the fetishized object of the gaze in the European movie house, Mai finds herself uncomfortably aligned with the norms of American confession within the dominant white American imaginary. Mai's refusal to speak confronts the confessional politics of visibility and voice, and resists the

Three. Fetish, Fantasy and Freedom

clean visibility and self-denying but vainglory of American voyeurism. Mai's refusal to confess *what it's like to be gang raped* in the *CBS* interview and her earlier rebuttal of anti–Pakistan sentiment are categorical rejections of colonial logic and an assertion of her own enlightened politicization, despite the perpetual framings of her as illiterate. Even though Mai's story gets picked up in the west in ways that appear to resonate with the strategic articulation of anti–Islamic narratives, Mai's voice (or silence) rejects this narrative and undercuts the paradigmatic discursive visual formation of brown women

It is also worth asking why other renowned women's rights cases in Pakistan were received so differently than Mukhtar Mai. Interestingly enough, during this time other rape cases were in motion in Pakistani judiciaries and medias. Veena Hayat, member of Pakistani political family and friend of Benazir Bhutto, was gang raped in 1991. Her story had some resonance in Pakistan because her family was politically connected. Her story, however, had little reaction in the west. Moreover, take the case of Shazia Khalid. Dr. Shazia Khalid, less a sensationalized figure than Mai, was raped by a Pakistani Army officer in 2005 on a military base where she was an onsite physician. Her rape surfaced quickly to the national press and then was just as quickly swept under the rug. Her case attracted publicity and outrage internationally only when then-President Musharraf proclaimed to an inter/national audience that "crying rape was an easy way for a Pakistani woman to make money and get a visa to Canada" (*CBC* 2006; *Washington Post* 2006). Eventually Khalid did obtain a visa to Great Britain, however, and left Pakistan with her husband and son and settled in London.

When Laura Bush, in a video tribute at the *Glamour* Magazine Banquet, (8 November 2005) says, "Please don't assume that it's only a story of heartbreak. Mukhtaran ... proves that one woman can really change the world" it is important to note how shifting the focus from a woman who fought the system and won (somewhat) to a woman who escaped to the suburbs of London (Shazia Khalid) challenges our understanding of U.S. power, human rights regimes and the interlaced notion of visual and narrative pleasure. Where now is the fantastic rage for the rape of Khalid? Where are her Western advocates when she is coerced into relocating from her home in Pakistan to the diasporas of Great Britain? In the field of human rights, there is perhaps no more important set of questions, given that the power of human rights resides in the "business of making visible acts of extreme cruelty" (Williams 2010, 35).

Will the Real Pakistani Woman Please Stand Up?

The gaping visual and discursive silence on Khalid's case raises interesting questions on which women become global symbols of human rights and which fall to the margins. Locating Khalid in the dominant gaze of human rights, it becomes quickly apparent that in the case of this Pakistani woman's rape, the proverbial shoe doesn't fit. Khalid's rape by a military official, her status as a doctor, as a wife, as a mother, her lack of visual presence in the inter/national press, and her eventual exodus from Pakistan, indict human rights visual regimes. Is it the crime that interests this regime, the act of sexual and physical violation that occurs against women across the globe, with soaring numbers in America; or is it the subject, a particular subject, that captivates this regime and, hence, the click of the camera?

Khalid's visual story lacks cinematic currency, with only few images of her available in all presses combined. *Associated Press*, for example, where I accessed and licensed many of the images for this book, had sixty-three images of Mai and none of Khalid. Khalid's rape was not a decree by feudal lords that demonstrate the backwardness of Pakistan but was by a military officer on a military base in which she was a medical practitioner. Her rape is too common to the U.S. state, which operates in a particular denial about its own military assaults on U.S. female soldiers. Khalid is not an "illiterate, peasant woman," descriptors often surrounding Mai, by whom the American woman may measure her literacy and worldliness. Khalid is an educated professional Pakistani woman living and practicing medicine inside the borders of Pakistan, disrupting the dominant U.S. and human rights imaginary on the feminine, racialized *other*. Even Musharraf's deeply troubling statement that catalyzed awareness (finally) around Khalid's rape fizzled out rapidly because it accessed a sublimated fear around immigration practices into the U.S. and Canada. Finally, Khalid unsuccessfully battled the system (with the help of the same activist and lawyer, Asma Jahangir) and eventually due to pressure from the military regime, left Pakistan and began a new life in London.

The invisibility of Khalid story juxtaposed to the hyper-visibility of Mai's story points to self-denial embedded in the contemporary merger of neoliberalism and human rights within global contexts. What I am pointing to here is how women's bodies and stories become the surface on which competing and shifting notions of freedom and oppression are screened within the realm of a paranoid, neoliberal global war. Both neoliberalism and human rights are fields that rely on particular discursive formations to promote themselves—the first resting on human intelligence, self-ownership and material acquisition and the latter on emotion, natural rights and a "state of being like us." Combined, these intelligent and emotional machines deny that, more than likely, contemporary human rights subjects are more likely to escape their confines, rather than reform it. That Khalid did just this alludes to the more rooted battle of human rights than the one that gets publicly acclaimed—that is, the battle to tear down the socio-ideological wall and to change society so that people will no longer desperately try to escape their own world. As Saba Mahmoud (in Scott 2008, 95) points out, "Any feminist concerned with improving Muslim women's lot, however, must begin not simply with the scorecard of Islam's abuses but the terms through which an act of violence is registered as worthy of protest, for whom, under what conditions, and toward what end."

Instead, in the 2006–2007 international field of human rights, Khalid disappears and Mai takes the stage. Her book, *In the Name of Honor*, was published in 2007 by Washington Square Press with a forward by Nicholas Kristoff. The cover photograph is not unlike **fig. 3**, evoking similar auratic tragedy but Mai is strategically dressed in white, her head-covering white, her gaze again directed away from the camera. The dichotomies through which these images are structured—between silence and speech, self-denial and self-fulfillment, Pakistan and America, local and the global—implicate Mai's story in a familiar teleological narrative of progress offered by the west. Both images operate as a means of persuasive pedagogy, demonstrating the process of disempowerment to empowerment, object to subject, victim to feminist. This kind of iconography sets into motion specific epistemic regimes that naturalize Pakistan as an oppressive state and (Western) visibility as a means of empowerment. Insofar as these photographs cannot be read separately from the Pakistan-American geopolitical transaction and the global war's vested gaze on the Pakistani female subject, the image becomes an event of cultural production, a moment in which "oppressed subjectivities" are constructed and free subjects are imagined. As the symbol of an indigenous imagination meeting liberal feminist normativization, both images of Mai reorder the audience's field of vision by rendering her intelligible, relevant, sensible. In the regime of visibility, oppression is something we can see, often on the body of women. The natural inverse, freedom, too, can be identified on the body, a point which becomes more apparent in my discussion of Benazir Bhutto.

The publication of Mai's book and its subsequent position in the *New York Times* bestseller list, speaks also to the "market" piece of human rights—its ironically capitalist dimensions. Mai's visualities are understood as redressing historical exclusions of dis/empowered Muslim women, however, they actually operate as essential to the diversification and reinvigoration of the dominant neoliberal culture and subject (Grewal 2005; Williams 2010). The tenuous reach of this dominant neoliberalization of human rights practices is curiously demonstrated in both the convincing images of victim/heroine binary and the rehabilitative strategies of human rights that follow, i.e., the publishing of her story (and now, Malala Yousafzai's) as the real Pakistani Woman. Human rights regimes appropriate and claim Mai's revolutionary feminist laboring within the common sensical, natural development of girls and women into autonomous, self-defining subjects. It is precisely this neutralization of Mai's revolutionary work into the spontaneously accepted human rights agenda that marks the power of this regime at its purest and its most effective. Asad (2003:158) sums up this elegantly when he says, "who is to be counted as human, what the capabilities are of the human subject, will be decided through the global market." If Mai is the modern Janus, in that she allows us to imagine a new beginning for real Pakistani women, in ways not even offered by her free counterpart, Benazir Bhutto, she also allows the dominant gaze to envision a primordial, ideal past subject while at the same time facing a modern future.

Beyond Pakistan: Portfolio of Brown Visual Subjects

As an ethical regime and a global rhetoric, human rights rely on tropes of risks as key to their discursive field. Vis-à-vis photographs and stories of the *other*, human rights insist on the brown woman subject as strikingly vulnerable and "at-risk." By representing the feminine, racialized *other* as a distinct population in need of charity and care of the West and through which she becomes a sovereign, autonomous subject; human rights meets a key tenet of Foucault's governmentality. In other words, this is where the brown woman becomes a global subject.

A provocative visual advertisement for a new documentary, entitled *Girls Rising*, captures this point. Co-sponsored by the Center for Women's

Health and Human Rights at Suffolk University and the Women's Forum at United Nations Association in Boston, *Girls Rising* (2013) is a "groundbreaking film which tells the stories of nine extraordinary girls from 9 countries, written by 9 celebrated writers, narrated by 9 renown actresses" (girlsrising.com). The visual image captures the faces of seven young brown girls, smiling and looking at the camera. All the girls in the photo ad are ethnicized either by hair, clothing or other aesthetic practices (e.g., *bindi*, a colorful Hindu dot on the forehead). Malala Yousafzai's photograph sits at the center of this image. The image and the documentary are directed at a largely white, U.S. audience. The ad for the film shares this epithet.

> Azmera is a 13-year-old Ethiopian who refused to be married and wanted to go to school instead. Although both her mother and grandmother were married at very young ages (10 and 11), Azmera dreamed of a different sort of life in which she could become a leader in her community instead of a child bride. "This is just what happens. There's no melodrama there. It's just a fact" [Maaza Mengiste, author of Azmera's story].

Operating within a deep genealogical genre of photography on the *other*, the text and image for the *Girls Rising* film functions as documentation. This notion of the photograph as a document of reality has been brought under scrutiny by a number of visual scholars, such as Barthes (1981), Tagg (1988), and McClintock (1995). But the familiar composition of brown women/girls cements U.S. ideas about what is real and what is artificial, what is reality and what is fantasy. The broader portfolio of feminine, racialized *others* as always and already oppressed trying to rise against all odds (like Mai or Malala), is certainly framed by a narrative of family strength and community support (in the case of Malala, her father and with Mai, the community of rural women); where (white) Westerners come across as progenitors of her international celebrity. Regardless, oppression gets representationally produced as quintessentially and exclusively "brown." In this next section, I will show how the visual culture that narrates these women relies on violently raced and sexed bodies (recall the *National Geographic* photo), reducing, even as it celebrates, these women to hyper-embodiment, in ways that, as I will show in later chapters, Bhutto tried to erase and the Lal Masjid women appeared to disembody.

On March 4, 2009, CARE sponsored an International Women's Day event, featuring an exclusive two-hour film of *Half the Sky* in 450 theatres in the U.S. and Canada. Nicholas Kristoff with Sheryl WuDunn published

Half the Sky: Turning Oppression into Opportunity (2009), where they explore what they call, "the rampant gendercide in the developing world." Featured on *Oprah, CNN News,* and *Dateline NBC, Half the Sky* has been on the *New York Times* bestseller list, has been used in women and gender studies courses and is a favorite across the globe. Tom Brokaw, a reviewer of the book, said: "the book's stories about real women will pierce your heart and arouse your conscience." Dr. Helene Gayle, president and CEO of CARE promoted the event, stating: "*Half the Sky* is more than just a night at the movies—it's a rallying cry to stand up and join a growing worldwide movement to empower women and girls to fight global poverty" (*CARE* Website ad, 4 March 2010). I was in Atlanta at the time, writing this particular chapter, ironically examining the visual devices of human rights discourse. Despite my ambivalence, I decided to attend the event.

Beginning with the epigraph, "changing the world one woman at a time," this film featured famous actresses such Marisa Tomei, well-known political figures, such as the Duchess of York, and showcased its proud sponsors, *Ladies Home Journal*, American Association of University Women, and WalMart, among others. The film opens with the story of Woineshet, a young rural Ethiopian girl who had been raped and forced into marriage with her rapist. Woineshet, in a pink dress, runs barefoot through dirt fields, past huts, laughing that innocent laughter reserved for children. We see her bare legs as they swing through the air with ease. Slowly, carefully, deliberately, the legs become heavy, the scene shifts from color to black and white, the pink dress suddenly tattered by the loss of color, the laughter turns into shrieks and large brown arms lift Woineshet's bare legs as she is taken, screaming.

Woineshet's story was enthralling in the way that it looped between reality and Hollywood dream, ultimately capturing the civic miracle of Woineshet's survival and promulgating the fetishization of brown women being saved from brown men by white men (Spivak 1988). Through a strategy of synecdochic substitutions, Woineshet's visual story represents the violent plight of all brown women. As synecdoche, these visual stories become the raison d'être of human rights. Indeed, the purpose of the film is not cast these women and girls as victims but just the opposite—as agents of their own liberation from the boundaries that constrict or oppress them. The simulation of sexual assault in the guise of moral righteousness confirms that human rights stories narrated through visual terrains hold provocative appeal.

Three. Fetish, Fantasy and Freedom

But the film nevertheless implies that the task of visually representing oppression is not just unproblematic, but worthy of commendation. For example, in the film premiere of *Half the Sky*, actress Marisa Tomei applauded Kristoff's column: "I thought to myself [after reading Kristoff's comments], are we really talking about women's issues, front and center, every day, every week? Yes, we are!" That the women's issues we were talking about are colored by race and nation yet unhinged from the paranoid practices that have brought them to Tomei's "front and center" is rendered conveniently invisible. Tomei's exclamatory words combined with the visual devices of the film normalize the social rhetoric and anxiety on brown women as oppressed and in need of protection, or as Uma Narayan (1997) provocatively phrases, "dead by culture."

As published versions of this (human rights) anxiety, *Half the Sky* reveals the sublimated vulgarity of human rights enterprises. In its quest for docile bodies turned neoliberal citizenship (Read: Woineshet, like Mai, is now "free" and speaking at International Women's day events around the world); the visual narrativization of Woineshet clearly fits in the broader struggle to advance human rights norms in the post–9/11 world. Discourses of rescue, particularly those emerging out of 9/11, become read through visibility, sexualized liberty, and entrance into political/civil spheres by the female subject/body (think here of *SATC2*). While the International Women's Day event aimed to draw attention to the "diagnostic" form of oppression for brown women, it nevertheless mobilized tropes of representation that are rooted in long histories of racialized violent colonialisms.

But the film conceals its ideological inflections with the seeming objectivity of human rights storytelling, appearing to the audience a benign depiction of simple (however, tragic) social fact. The heavy-handed style, visually as well as narratively, centralizes the fetishistic interest in brown women's human rights. On aesthetic grounds, this film of Woineshet's abduction can be condemned for its derivativeness, vulgar sentimentality, garishness and crass simplicity. On ideological grounds, this cinematic moment is part of a commercial culture industry that feeds off the credulity and ignorance of the American liberal-ish masses, elucidating the lexicon of a paranoid empire. Every detail in this film is strategic, weaving together the benevolence of human rights that determine Woineshet as (now) free and the paranoid technologies that magnify, manipulate and multiply images of (oppressed) brown bodies.

Time magazine's August 2010 popular and controversial cover makes this point abundantly clear. The cover depicts the photograph of a young Afghani woman, Bibi Aisha, a purple shawl draped over her hair, whose nose is mutilated because "her nose and ears were cut off by Taliban for fleeing abusive in-laws" (9 August 2010, http://www.npr.org/blogs/thetwo-way/2010/10/13/130527903/bibi-aisha-disfigured-afghan-woman-featured-on-time-cover-visits-u-s). The cover boldly reads, "What happens if we leave Afghanistan." It is not a question, but a statement. The photograph was awarded the World Press Photo of the Year, one of the highest honors in photojournalism.

As a site of both political fantasy, in that this woman's disfigured face justifies the war, and violent excess, as such forms of violence are disavowed by the U.S. heteronormative state, this photograph operates as a crucial site of American spectatorship on the war and human rights. Here, the figure of woman is pervasively instrumental in shifting the function of discursive systems, wherein she becomes the signifier of the unsuccessful democratic nation-state and the war on terror becomes part of the natural evolution to women's-rights-as-human-rights. This photograph, similar to the *National Geographic* image but much more severe, abstracts and reifies a feminine, racialized o*ther* in need of varying measures of benevolence, while also buoying paranoia.

What's important to note is that Bibi Aisha was mutilated in "liberated" Afghanistan—that is Afghanistan under control of Karzai and the U.S. and not in the Taliban controlled areas. This important bit of information was missing, or was downplayed, from much of the coverage of the incident in the U.S. press. Further, Taliban denied responsibility of this act. We know that they always claim responsibility for their acts (no matter how horrific, the attempted assassination of 14-year-old Malala Yousafzai exemplifies this). Also, Aryan Baker, the journalist who wrote the article has a personal connection to ISAF (International Security Assistance Force)—her husband. Her husband, Tamim Samee, an Afghan-American IT entrepreneur, is a board member of an Afghan government minister's $100 million project advocating foreign investment in Afghanistan, and has run two companies, Digistan and Ora-Tech, that have solicited and won development contracts with the assistance of the international military, including private sector infrastructure projects favored by U.S.-backed leader Hamid Karzai. In other words, *Time* reporter Aryn Baker who wrote story of Bibi Aisha, bolstering the case for war, appears to have benefited materially from the NATO invasion. *Time* defended its cover story as neither in support of, nor in opposition to, the U.S. war effort but rather a "straightforward reported piece" (Gorenfield 2010).

The power and legitimacy of this photograph marks a neocolonial schema that produces indifference in fact, while inciting paranoid fantasy rooted in little to no reality. For example, much of the American public appeared indifferent to the fact that both the Afghan and Iraqi regimes targeted by Bush had previously been supported by or even built by earlier U.S. foreign policy. It also appeared indifferent to the touting of the "liberation" of Afghan women as one of the greatest achievements of the overthrow of the Taliban while the overthrow of the Baath regime set into motion an immediately more oppressive regime of gender in Iraq (Brown 2005). As I've noted, the war in Afghanistan was presented by the American media not only as against terrorists but also as for the liberation of Afghan women. Hence, Aisha's tragedy remained relevant, winning journalistic awards and prompting conversation from coffeehouses to academic classrooms.

Apart from the political service the image performs, in denuding Aisha of historical and personal context, the image strips Muslim women of moral intelligence and erases their participation in democratic aspirations of their homeland, reducing them into colonial harem context. The visual production of Aisha, like all brown bodies of human rights interest, extends beyond its actual physicality, situating her as an object of cultural value in a technologically-mediated postmodern and imperial world, further punctuated by the forces of transnational networks and processes (Appadurai 1996). Aisha's body, and largely the bodies of racialized and colonized women that have come in contact with the imperial camera, is/are produced as spectacle/s by the machinations of power and pleasure that sit at the foundation of American interest (Zita 1998). Aisha's (un)free body is restored as a body that matters, a discursive representation of human rights that is more real than (her) reality.

Raison d'Être: Human Rights Visual Culture as Erotic Panopticon

Foucault (1982), in *Discipline in Punish,* explains that the panopticon was the architectural design of French prison in which each prisoner and prison staff could be monitored. He describes the theme of the panopticon as "at once surveillance and observation, security and knowledge, individualization and totalization, isolation and transparency" (217). While this analysis is directed at prisons, Foucault acknowledges how the panopticon metaphor extends into systems of education, medicine, psychiatry, etc. The theory behind the panopticon was that not only should the delinquent's behaviors and movements be observed but the observations should trace back to his motivations, his psychological viewpoints, social positions and upbringings in order to understand any and all proclivities (Foucault 1977: 221). Foucault's (1977) panopticon operates as a central metaphor for the modern production of bodies subjected to multiple spectral and omnipresent surveillance techniques, fundamentally "normalizing bodies." But alongside this production of *seen* bodies, as I suggested in the previous chapter, meanings of the body are partly produced in a semiotically infused physical exchange of erotic energy between object-looked-upon and the adoring/disgusted gaze (Rose 2007; Zita 1998; Mulvey 1977). Hence, I want to position Foucault's original panopticon as one that is erotic, in that functions to express, direct, and produce desire for the *other*.

The erotic panopticon discursively produces a feminine, corporeal Muslim nation-state by successive waves of inciting a pleasurable nostalgia around women's bodies as violable, victim, and virtuous. As hyper-represented bodies in the U.S. media, narrowing geopolitical complexities into visual nuggets of alternating *jouissance* and fear, these photographs function to pleasure the viewer viscerally and voyeuristically. Whether it is Mai, Woineshet or Aisha, the feminine racialized *other* is more often read less through her subjectivity and more through her brown female body—mythic, hyper-oppressed and simultaneously hyper-enabled. Taking place in the most visual of registers, these visual subjects oscillate between free and unfree, sustaining and suspending (brown) danger and (white) security, swinging our gaze back and forth.

Let me elaborate here. A curious logic belies the humanitarianism underscoring Mai's specific story, one that is closely linked to narratives of colonial exceptionalism and the female body. Through the repeated display of Mai's body that tells us she is (not) free—**fig. 3** is the most widely circulated image of Mai, despite all the work she has done since her assault—we become privy to the neocolonial/neoliberal imperatives that determine her practice(s), her "self," and her body as oppressed. These corporealities not only elucidate the lexicon of American control but also demonstrate the increasing fascination of human rights narratives in Muslim women's bodies and practices around the body. For example, Nicholas Kristoff writes a biweekly oped for the *New York Times* about women "like" Mai. Kristoff has certainly been a voice that has helped bring attention to oppression and sexual violence against women globally, yet his well-intentioned reporting often positions him as a savior figure oblivious to his privilege as a (heterosexual) white male, and whitewashes the complex histories of these communities. In the case of Mai, for Kristoff (2009:76), a sign of Mai's path towards liberation was when she shook hands with American men and realized "the world will not end if her scarf drops." The contortions of logic and rhetoric that characterize these attempts to define empowerment testify to a total lack of recognition of their imperialist stance, which constructs the essentially paternalistic and sexualized project of American representations of the *other*.

Kristoff (2010), in his discussion of women's oppression in the developing world, displays an incessant need to physically describe the women. For example, in his chapter title, "Microcredit: The Financial Revolution," he describes two Pakistani women (one educated at Wharton, the other at Mount Holyoke) who "wanted to save the world, and so they joined the World Bank." He describes these women as a "striking pair: well-educated, well-connected, well-dressed and beautiful" (189). Identity formation draws upon the image of the *other*. James Clifford (1988, 2) has argued that the content of the category of non-Western or "primitive" changes over time, but is consistently used to construct an alter ego or confirm the Western self. This relationship between aesthetics and politics, one I take up seriously in the following chapter, at the very least suggests a theoretical and political dissonance with what Kristoff conceptualizes to be representations for self and social empowerment.

Clearly, racial conditions continue to apply in understandings and treatments of the human body, as in Kristoff's framing of Mai's liberation, in cultural and public practices, and in patterns of aesthetics and normalcy. So, just as Kristoff is pleased with Mai's "liberatory" practice of shaking hands with men and her dupatta slipping off to reveal her hair, her broken display after her assault incites a different form of pleasure, one we see at the nexus of eroticism and violence. It seems, unfortunately, Kristoff can only see women of color through the lens of victimization and struggle.

As an eroticized victim of a high profile crime, Mai's figure operates somewhat similarly to the eroticization of high-profile crimes in America. Writing about the ways high profile crimes become hotbeds of social causes, Chancer (2005) argues that such crimes operate as cultural events that, for better or worse, give concrete expression to latent social conflicts in American society. Chancer explores how criminal cases become conflated with larger social causes on a collective level, "producing wrought ambivalent effects on social movements simultaneous to pleasure and satisfaction in the spectator" (2005:78). Chancer's point is relevant here. On the one hand, Mai's high profile rape offers important opportunities for emotional expression and raises awareness of social issues. On the other hand, it confounds the American-Pakistan geopolitical nexus, taps into the pleasures incited by eroticized violence, and meshes race and sex fantasies onto the body of the Pakistani woman subject.

Fig. 3 of Mai is a provocative example of an image that communicates the affective essence of pleasure (through eroticized violence). This stylized, emotionally graphic, starkly colored photograph intended to depict a woman brutalized by sexual assault, is interlaced with an eroticization of the brown, female body. Every detail in this display is ideological even as it appears to have captured Mai in her most organic state. Mai's affirmative positioning in the American media and her hyper-enabled Pakistani feminine and feminist traversal taps into an American erotic imagination that fantasizes about supernormal. Mai stabilizes in the American imaginary a (brown) woman who is pure, loyal, modest, forgiving, patient—the balancing symbolism of womanhood but also a super hero in her ability to take on an unimaginable oppressive national system—Pakistan.

One of the most compelling and redeeming features of Mai, as an internationalized visual story, is her indigenousness—the reading of her body as naturally and normatively Pakistani (similar to the *National Geographic* image). This reality is produced palpably (for the viewer) by the physical and feminine sublimity of Mai's photographs. She becomes the means through which the dominant imaginary visualizes, disciplines and inscribes difference, a visuality that relies on both the surface of the body and the conduct of the new empowered subject. Her photographs provide a visual and conceptual fusion of repression meeting emancipation. Through her, a new, neoliberal mode of social perception is established, a way of disciplining difference and making it socially usable, desirable, satisfactory. Militarized, hetero-patriarchal capitalism thrives on practices of social erasure and social visibility—by restoring Mai, the market emerges as liberator par excellence. This avowal of Mai, despite the mark of deviant sex (her gang rape), allows the American gaze the specular pleasure of seeing Mai, within the dominant paradigm of femininity, as virtuous but violable, chaste but inevitably carnal, good but aphrodisiacal. Ultimately, **fig. 3** of Mai, in its hyper-circulation, restores the violence against her even as it attempts to posit her as an agentic subject.

Laura Mulvey (1977) tells us that woman is conventionally fetishized into cultural material verbally and visually (as vulnerable, violable). In the case of *Time* magazine's controversial image, this semiotic fact is a starting point in Aisha's (*Time* magazine) photograph, but it is not its finishing point.

> She was so beautiful that the first time I saw Bibi Aisha on the cover of *Time* magazine it took me a moment to realize she didn't have a nose. Her husband and his family had hacked it off when she'd tried to escape being abused in her home. The magazine said she was the graphically horrifying illustration for the fate that awaits many women if the U.S. withdraws from Afghanistan too soon [www.npr.com 10 October 2010].

The photograph elicits a response from the spectator that is not just political (war as a means to save) but also erotic (Aisha as object of beauty), becoming a visual site through which power and pleasure are sought, distributed, and confirmed. *Time,* then, is not just using women to uphold a political and ideological view that supports militarism. It is also using feminine beauty and the patriarchal fear of and disgust for deformed women to sell an agenda. Indeed, few things are more offensive to a society that privileges the visual than seeing a beautiful woman horribly disfigured. The fact that "Aisha was once an attractive girl with luscious black hair and piercing eyes" adds to the horror and disturbing nature of the cover.

Jodi Bieber, the award-winning photographer who took Aisha's picture, talks about her approach in making the iconic photograph of Aisha in an interview (www.time.com, 29 July 2010). She says, "I could have made a photograph with her looking or being portrayed more as the victim," Beiber says. "And I thought, no, this woman is beautiful." *NPR*'s Karen Bates' statement similarly romanticizes Aisha's beauty. The use of hetero-erotic language to describe Aisha, arguably, is merely a narrative trope that allows the viewer to know her and feel aligned with her. But this framing of Aisha as beautiful (and this beauty as an accidental prize for the spectator) misses the more nuanced eroticism embedded in using women's bodies to justify war. The sexually loaded trope of describing Aisha as attractive, and then mourning the loss of that same attractiveness, signifies the erotic gaze embedded in gazing at (brown) women who've been victims of violence. This tension between the fetishized spectacle of brown women's bodies and the violence to which they are subjected generated both erotic fantasy and politico-cultural disgust.

In an interview at the Victoria Albert Museum as part of a series called "Real Beauty" (viemeo.com, 20 March 2011), Bieber states: "I could never imagine how she feels, never ever, but there is a moment of healing and just by saying she's beautiful something happened within her. And I said look at the camera, and I said feel something, you know, feel your beauty and that's the photograph I got." However self-conscious and empowering Bieber attempts to be, she is restricted to a formal *mise en scene* reflecting the dominant ideological concept of visualizing the *other*. By placing Aisha, along with other human rights subjects, in the category of the *other*, a position both injurious and inherently unstable—freedom comes to be defined through relation to whiteness as a fantasy (e.g., such atrocities manifest at a distance from the white imaginary). Both Aisha and Mai's body, then, is situated at the intersection of a number of significant determinants—race, nation, class, gender, sexuality, violence, ability—but their ethereal quality is entwined with a life story that hails the American dream, a dream envisaged through the (brown) female body.

The photographic portfolio displaying brown women as victims of exceptional forms of sexual/gender violence—violence, which is fetishistically reproduced and disavowed by the U.S. state (read: Abu-Ghraib) demarcates a political climate obsessed with feminized, nativized and racialized *others*. Insofar as the intrigue in these visual subjects is constituted through a hetero-patriarchal gaze that frames their violence as an eroticized, sensationalized, fantasized spectacle of their (brown) nation, these women, I argue, come to embody an *erotic national*. The erotic national can be understood as photographed subjects whose gendered and nativized positions are consistently underwritten by a neocolonial sexualization of the *other*, which then, cannot be separated from white neoliberal, multicultural efforts to render them *real* subjects of their (brown) nation. In using the term, erotic national, I recognize that human rights frameworks overwhelmingly present themselves as international, however, the subjects in whom human rights takes an interest are articulated through narrativizations of the (masculine) state, (feminine) self, and (paranoid) international security. The erotic subjectivity, then, afforded these women is the simultaneous effect of the national and the international, Empire's benevolence and paranoia, all of which come together to name these feminine bodies and subjectivities as tragic but triumphant, beaten but beautiful, damaged but desirable.⁵

Human rights discourses do attempt to challenge hetero-erotic and patriarchal readings of the female body, but even as they challenge this, they, too, mobilize it. In part, the work is already done by the cultural misogyny in place that creates, despises, and eroticizes violence against women. Insofar as human rights discourses cannot contain this seductive reading of the feminine, racialized *other*, it relentlessly uses it to promulgate its rhetoric. As an eminent body of knowledge on free and oppressed subjectivities, human rights regimes have captured our imagination through a mastery of symbols of brown women's bodies and incantation of free, white bodies. This emphasis on brown, sexualized bodies haunts human rights photography and, as Leela Fernandez (2013:118) argues, in her critique of regimes of visibility, "the deeper questions regarding the relationship between power and knowledge become reduced to visible textual strategies of representation." The visual practices around Mai, Aisha and the International Women's Day film are meant to capture the sadistic, violent patriarchy of the *other* (and the possibilities of the feminine racialized *other* experiencing liberation) but the *hetero-eroticism* of human rights photography is also revealed, cracking the masquerade of freedom and revealing power relations threaded with colored and sexualized bodies.

From Mai to Malala: Infantalizing Pakistani Feminist Labor

When I began considering the possibility of writing a chapter on the use of visual culture by mainstream human rights enterprises, Mai was the most dominant figure emerging out of Pakistan. From *Glamour* to the *New York Times*, the discourses surrounding her swung like a pendulum, articulating barbaric nations, corrupt Pakistani politics, Mai's individual exceptionalism, and the power of U.S. visibility. I was compelled to interrogate this discursive field through the vector of visual culture, reacting to the gaping silence on how brown women's bodies are used to construct simple and accessible epistemologies of the *other*, servicing (intended or not) the white racial state.

I was finishing the final touches on this chapter, when news of

Will the Real Pakistani Woman Please Stand Up?

Malala Yousafzai's attempted assassination by the Taliban took over the global media, exhibiting a fresher and younger version of violence against women in Pakistan. Unlike the violence perpetrated on Mukthar Mai, which framed her as feudal, illiterate, and victim; Malala, at the age of 14, emerged as educated, empowered and determined. And while Mai's perpetrators were abstract symbols of Pakistan's tight feudal patriarchy, Malala's violent experience was an emblematic Taliban slaughter, where they took great pride in their work. From displaying her face on TV screens across North American malls to the widespread coverage of her survival and her determining words on popular television shows like the *Daily Show*, Malala quickly became a household name in the U.S. and, I would venture to guess, throughout the Western world. She became, in a word, the face of the Pakistani women's rights movement, despite the fact that she was and in fact, still is a young girl.

The fact that Malala is seen as the ultimate symbol of Pakistan's failure towards girls and the only form of hyper-secularized feminism imagined in Pakistan has the dual effect of racializing Islam and erasing the multi-faceted feminist work that has always been part of Pakistani cultural and political fabric. The significance of Malala's assault for many Westerners is that it raised a lot more awareness about the prevalence of the opposition to the education of girls that exists in many places around the world. But the idea that somehow the rest of the world beyond U.S. and Europe is not educating its girls is not only false but a key colonial narrative. In contrast, the idea that Islam and Muslims prevent girls from getting an education is, too, far from a neutral construction. The colonial deployment of Malala is used to reinforce the idea that Muslims are barbaric, uneducated, oppressive to women and prevent them from getting an education.

Like Mai, I saw Malala as a media toy created and financed generously to construct Pakistan and Muslims in highly offensive terms, however in this case, with the complicity of her family. In Pakistan and in South Asia in general it is well known how she was mounted into an international symbol and that her entire family is getting rich off it. Malala supposedly stands in for how badly Muslim countries and Muslims in general treat their girls. However, the Pakistan government (where she is from) provides free education for all children and youth and has all kinds of campaigns and programs specifically to promote girls' education, including door to door campaigns, announcements on billboards and buses promoting girls education, urban and rural teachers where needed,

Three. Fetish, Fantasy and Freedom

and a whole apparatus with punishments and rewards. The attack on Malala's right to an education, if indeed there was one, is from an extremist group in Pakistan, something like the KKK in the U.S., after which a huge international hullaballoo was made about it. Malala, however, is being used in many quarters of the world to reinforce Islamophobia, which then works to legitimize the Western governments' invasions of Muslim countries, which results in the slaughter of the population including women and children and the devastation of its entire economy, infrastructure, present and future. Indeed, Malala, like so many of the human rights subjects in this chapter, falls right into the colonial trope that Gayatri Spivak (1988) identifies as "white men—and white women—save brown women from brown men."

Furthermore, the idea that suddenly a girl, Malala, is the first Muslim woman to ever work for Muslim women's rights is an enormously oppressive and inaccurate construction. There is a longstanding feminist movement in Pakistan, much of which the Western media has taken little to no interest in.[6] Malala, as the symbol of women's struggle in Pakistan, elides four decades of women's rights activism and feminist labor in Pakistan. Within the discourses of Malala (and Mai) lurks the reality of Pakistani feminist labor—labor dated to Pakistan's inception in 1947 insofar as women have always participated in nationalist independence movements, but more directly to 1979, with the onset of General Zia's deeply gendered regime which catalyzed the formation of Tehrik-e-Niswan (The Women's Movement), Women's Action Forum and The Aurat (Women's) Foundation. These women's individual and organizational activism engages in feminist work that cut across all sectors of civil society—education, health, poverty, domestic violence, rape, and the denial of rights, including legal/political reform, such as the 2006 groundbreaking legal dissolutions of the Hudood Ordinances to more creative forms of feminist labor such as, Tehrik-e-Niswan performance of street theatre in Karachi to foster dialogues around gender, sexuality and reproductive rights. The use of street theatre and dramatic performance is intended to suffuse cultural narratives with counter stories on both women's dignity around health, education and family rights as well as stake out a discursive space for voices of young, marginalized girls.

But this elision is not the only sin. The hegemonic circulation of Malala as the iconic fighter of women's education and rights in Pakistan infantalizes the Pakistani feminist movement, its adult movers and shakers and reinstates the political valence that feminism must be taught to

Pakistani women, in this case by a brave young Malala, who now lives in the West. This paternalism has racial and gender coordinates. Malala is a Pakistani young girl who becomes particularly interesting (to the West) through surviving violence done to her, through a public claim to social injury—Pakistani girls' inability to safely access education. The use of her age as a transfer point between being the disempowered Pakistani female to believing she can access empowerment and rights (outside of Pakistan) reveals a startling contradiction. Malala's vulnerabilities pivot around age, nation, gender and class, yet these same vectors in conjunction with one another open up the possibilities for her agency. She is, theoretically, the perfect humanist subject. Gayatri Spivak's (2012:166) point resonates here, "the most frightening thing about imperialism, its long term toxic effect, what secures it, what cements it, is the benevolent self-representation of the imperialist as savior."

With the ubiquitous and tyrannical visual configurations that imagine Pakistani women and girls as subject to forms of violence disavowed by the U.S. state, trying to find a model that adds complexity to the lived experiences of Pakistani women's lifeworlds feels impossible. If the role of young girls in Pakistan under the dual thumbs of patriarchy and empire is to learn lessons of gender oppression and white/Western superiority, Malala beautifully fails, enacting Halberstam's (2010) poignant reframing of failure as a queer site of resistance. But in the formal spaces of the visual and discursive media world, even the images of Malala contribute to the fiction of U.S. empire, hiding U.S. violence in plain sight, shifting it to narrative aporias.

The violent (brown) images and narratives that dominate the international human rights theatre and the violence of these (brown) images and narratives do not operate on different fields, but the latter requires a counter-narrative to which I hope this book will contribute. I offer a reading of these human rights figures that complicates and troubles visual witnessing and admits, with a sigh, that here, too, the specter of the photograph hovers. In order to fight atrocity, it has to be exposed. Regardless of their ethical value, as jouissance or restitution, these visualities participate in practices of power that do less to fight atrocity and more to sustain the powers through which these atrocities are enacted.

Four

Is There a Queer Democracy? Or—Stop Looking Straight
Benazir Bhutto and the Hetero-Erotics of Democracy

Instead of interrogating a category, we will interrogate a woman. It will at least be more agreeable.
—Denise Riley, 1988, 35

I do not paint a portrait to look like the subject; rather does the person grow to look like [her] portrait.
—Salvador Dali, 1943

On December 27, 2007, Benazir Bhutto, the leader of Pakistan's largest political party, was killed. I was in Pakistan at the time of her death, attending a family wedding in Karachi. I had just come from an intense day and half conference in Lahore ironically titled "Pakistan in the Global (Dis) Order." I sat with several of my cousins at a women's salon, when one woman came running into the room, weeping, saying that Bhutto had been killed. My cousins and I didn't believe it. We agreed that Bhutto was killed off every day by her foes, only to emerge alive and lovely as always. But indeed, the young girl was correct and we were quickly shooed out of the salon so they could shut their doors before the riots broke out. On our way home, our driver quickly informed us as he raced

Will the Real Pakistani Woman Please Stand Up?

through the densely-packed, narrow streets of Clifton, a Karachi neighborhood, that the roads were dangerous, the people angry, and the city would soon go mad. My cousins and I, all part of the Pakistani diaspora that left Karachi a decade or more back and settled in varying parts of the U.S and U.K., again scoffed. The city would mourn, indeed, but political madness among the masses? That was an urban legend.

Again, we stood corrected. Within two hours, violent uprisings and protest in the forms of arson and killings swept through the nation, predominantly in Karachi, which was known as Bhutto's most loyal city. Stories of car and bus burnings, government offices set ablaze, civilians pulled out of cars and beaten, and store lootings rang in everyone's ears as the nation sat glued to the few working channels on television. In a matter of minutes, the entire city of Karachi was shut down, wedding receptions and parties canceled, businesses closed, stores padlocked, military officials arrived on main roads ordered to shoot on sight any miscreant behavior. The country had officially gone into mourning.

Unprepared for a three-day city shutdown, we had all headed to a two bedroom flat in the heart of the city, already occupied by extended family. And so I sat with twenty or so extended family and friends, entranced and devastated by her death and even more by the aftermath of her assassination. The political madness that hit the streets within hours of her murder covered TV screens, instilling fear, trepidation and awe. The street violence that followed Bhutto's murder was a powerful testimonial to Fanon's[1] (1963) contribution on violent corporeal agency—the only agency afforded to the colonized. His tragic accuracy politicized and saddened me. These Fanonian readings intercepted my thoughts, compelling me to understand how, caught up in the spiral of history, these dispossessed subjects of globalization trigger/ed change through the echo of violence.

I sat with my family, listening to tales of Bhutto's manipulative endeavors, her phoniness, the hatred towards her pro–Western rhetoric, the hypnosis of her rhetoric. "She was beautiful," someone said. And "smart shrewd actually,"[2] another voice chimes in. Her death is poetic justice, they agree, deserved. She had laid herself bare as a target, beckoning her enemies with her pro–Western stance, her hyper secularism and perhaps, even her femaleness. But, Moon must have loved her, someone said. They all turned to me. After all, she was a woman and I was a feminist.

I open this chapter with this memory of the evening of Bhutto's

Four. Is There a Queer Democracy? Or—Stop Looking Straight

death to show that there are many ways to talk about Bhutto. While there is no unified narrative of events that capture Benazir Bhutto's return to Pakistan's political scene, nor a disengaged objective recital of facts that detail her political work, there are a series of common facts that require articulation in order to establish her importance to feminist discourses around the globe. Benazir Bhutto, a prominent political leader of the Peoples' Party of Pakistan (PPP), was often depicted as the symbol of democracy by both Western political discourses and Pakistani national politics. She was overwhelmingly read by both political discourses in Pakistan and in the West as the solution to Pakistan's national crisis, in terms of resisting the rise of Islamization and developing a democratic nation-state.

Born in 1953, Benazir Bhutto was reared in Pakistani politics under her father, Zulfiqar Ali Bhutto, who founded the Peoples Party of Pakistan (PPP); presiding over Pakistan from 1971–1977, until he was charged with political corruption and murder, and publicly hung in 1979. Benazir Bhutto became the nation's and the Muslim world's first female prime minister in 1988. Twice elected to and twice expelled from that office, she spent much of her later life in exile, battling charges of alleged corruption. The dismissals typified her volatile political career, which was characterized by numerous peaks and troughs. Bhutto's return to the Pakistani political scene after the events of September 11, 2001, was catalyzed by a rising distrust in the Musharraf regime both by national parties and Western political forces—the U.S. emerged as a key figure in encouraging her reentry. The U.S. powers saw Bhutto as a popular leader with liberal leanings who could bring much needed legitimacy to Musharraf's role in the war against terror. Hence, Bhutto reentered Pakistan in 2007, a year that has been named the most violent in Pakistani history. Her reentry was marked by violence from the start, ending with her assassination on the 27th of December 2007. *BBC* (www.bbc.com, 27 December 2007) tells us, "Benazir Bhutto followed her father into politics, and both of them died because of it, he was executed in 1979, she fell victim to an apparent suicide bomb attack."

Oft compared to the Nehru-Gandhi family in India and the Kennedys in America, the Bhuttos of Pakistan are one of the world's most famous—and troubled—political dynasties. The questionable nature of Bhutto's politics remains largely in the margins of global political discourse—her decision to remain married to Asif Zardari, even though there were rumors of adultery, violence and possible divorce, the charges of corruption rooted in part in her extravagant spending, the will/letter where she leaves PPP to her minor son which left Zardari head of the party and eventual president of Pakistan after her assassination, where he was basically unpopular but tolerated by the U.S. because it was generally believed that he was their yes-man. The *American Prospect* (*prospect.org*, 31 December 2007), a liberal American political magazine, describes Bhutto:

> To the West at large, she spoke the language of secular democracy. To American women, Bhutto spoke the language of feminism, filling a void left by the absence of a female American counterpart to mirror her ascent to power in Pakistan.

Amidst this, Benazir Bhutto emerged as the most elaborate articulation of Pakistan's modernity. Photographs and stories of her dominated the front covers of media in the U.S. and in Pakistan itself, as both nations struggled to make or deny space for this female political leader. According to *BBC* (27 December 2007), "at the height of her popularity, shortly after her first election, she was one of the most high-profile women leaders in the world." With vacillating descriptions of "young and glamorous," to "a successful and refreshing contrast to the overwhelmingly male-dominated political establishment," Benazir Bhutto, albeit unevenly and contradictorily, ascended into the global gaze as political spectacle, feminist symbol, democracy's icon, and modernity's emblem.

In this chapter, I am concerned with the representational imagery and narration that positioned Bhutto as a visual form of democracy and modernity that was fashioned with and functioned towards particular power modalities. As I've argued throughout this book, representations are never irrelevant, never unconnected to the world of actual social and power relations. I locate Bhutto as a feminine, racialized *other* successfully folded into the West's modern democratic embrace, a success in part achieved by de-racializing her. The political and cultural labyrinth in which she was caught and through which she came to be both symbol and spectacle speaks to the subtleties of empire that work to render the *other* palatable. In examining her appropriation by the west and visual culture's role in that appropriation, I work to move Bhutto from the dominant uncontested optical regime to a complexly textured discursive field that conceals many different corporeal desires and (geo)political depths. In queering the space between Bhutto and democracy, between Bhutto and empowerment, my attempt is perhaps to make something queer happen to the signified—Bhutto's body—and the signifier—to language and representation. Fundamentally, I underscore the precariousness of Bhutto and draw attention to the limits of the conventions and rules of freedom that were advanced through her. To deconstruct Bhutto is to demystify the exposure she received, to uncover the material interests at stake in her symbolization, to reveal the ideologies that held her in place, and to ask: through Bhutto, what forms of democracy and liberation advanced? What forms were deferred, displaced, defeated?

Ideological Topographies: Bhutto as Fantasy and (U.S.) Politics

Situating Benazir Bhutto in the discursive dilemmas that constituted her post–9/11 reentry into Pakistani politics and her automatic specularity in the dominant and sub-dominant global gaze requires a deliberate critical gesture that examines the language and visualities through which Bhutto came to be, arguably, Pakistan's most spectacular subject. One of the chief sources of the in/appropriation of Bhutto in the global political theatre lies in the way she was consigned to visuality. This consignment is the result of an epistemological mechanism which produces social difference vis-à-vis bodies and which (post)modernism magnifies with the availability of visual realities (Mirzeoff 1998; Sontag 2000; Hawley 2001).

To begin, I want to highlight an excerpt from an article written on Bhutto in the *American Prospect,* on the day of her assassination. Adele Stan (2007), writing for the *American Prospect* (Stan 2007) states:

> From the moment she appeared on the international scene, she was destined to be an icon. To the West, Benazir Bhutto, the first democratically-elected woman to lead a Muslim nation, looked like a Disney drawing of a beautiful fairytale princess from an animated fable set somewhere in the mysterious Orient.

This description edifies the foreign gaze, producing both itself as a species of rhetoric and Bhutto as an object of American fascination, replete with fragments of the past, the trappings of the modern, and fantasies of the hyperreal. At the very least, the *Prospect's* description of Bhutto yields cognitive dissonance with her as democratic, feminist figure (of a Muslim nation, no less). But, if we, like Foucault (1977) and Derrida (1983) consider language, that is to say, discourse—as a modality of power, then we see how this excerpt repositions Bhutto as a symbolic machine and an abstract subject who came to play a significant role in neocolonial *jouissance*, democracy's fantasy and the hetero-erotic gaze. Through such a narrativization, Bhutto is reduced to a kind of discursive game, one in which she serves as the link in a political economy that hinges on enjoying particular feminine corporealities and fantasizing about specific forms of neocoloniality.

The language of the *Prospect*, "somewhere in the mysterious Orient" speaks to an American fantasy that relies on the construction of an *other* who signifies a premodern, topographic distance whose crevices cannot be traced, whose depth is unmapped, unknown but desired. For a moment, this description of the feminine *other*, as Mulvey (in Jones 1993) notes, allows the spectator to imagine the *other* as powerful. The description of Bhutto as aesthetically beautiful and politically powerful through a recognizable and desirable political enterprise renders her "far away" distance closer through the familiar language of democracy and Western beauty. But this power is quickly neutralized by specific semantic conventions that reduce women to their gazed-upon bodies. The contradictions in the *Prospect's* statement speak to both the desire felt toward the feminine, racialized *other* simultaneous with a desire to construct (through political enterprise) the desirable modern *other*. This excerpt hints at what Mulvey (in Jones 1993:52) refers to as fetishistic scopophilia, the "pleasure in looking at another person as an erotic object." Again, I am not implying that images of Bhutto are the same as erotic pictures. By extending Mulvey's point to Bhutto's visual story, I argue that a fetishistic scopophillia, in varied manifestations, is embedded in heteropatriarchal imperial politics, which builds up the physical beauty of the female object, transforming it into something satisfying in itself (Mulvey in Jones 1993).

Correlative to the metaphors woven into the description of Bhutto are the images through which the world came to *see* and know Bhutto. The photograph that accompanies the *Prospect* article (**see fig. 4**) is of a candlelight vigil held by her female supporters in Lahore, Pakistan. In the foreground, we see a poster of Bhutto as a young Prime Minister (rather than of her as an older oppositional candidate of Musharraf, which is the context of her assassination). The picture is of Bhutto's face—her face is tilted upwards, her complexion is immaculate. She is looking forward, her mouth turned upwards in a slight smile, a white headscarf loosely frames her face, and diamond earrings glitter from under her hair. Her posture, the tilted face, the empowered demeanor, the glossy but

Four. Is There a Queer Democracy? Or—Stop Looking Straight

Figure 4. Supporters of Pakistan's slain opposition leader Benazir Bhutto hold candles during a ceremony marking the end of the 40-day mourning period in Lahore, Pakistan, on February 7, 2008 (AP Photo/Emilio Morenatti).

serious expression, the perfectly applied makeup all reveal, consciously and unconsciously, the social structures in which Bhutto was embedded and the ways in which her body came to symbolize the hinge through which Pakistan would swing open its doors to democracy. Bhutto's disposition in the poster is largely anglicized, e.g., her fair-toned skin is almost translucent in the image, organizing the ways in which she exudes Western power simultaneous to Pakistani nationalism. In line with Prospect's description, William Darwymple (2007) of the *Huffington Post*, names Bhutto, "Pakistan's flawed and feudal princess." Bhutto, all tropes in order, emulates both nation and empire.

There is thus an aesthetics at the core of politics that we see emerging out of Bhutto's visual story. The necessary conflation of her aesthetics with democracy that the passage suggests implicates beauty, within mainstream discourse, as not only a feminine standard or goal, but as a mechanism of power that reproduces class positions and racist stereotypes. As Eisenstein (2007) argues, stylizing images of the *other* is decisive to empire building. The symbolic appropriation of Bhutto as democratic and as free is crucial to maintaining race, gender and class distinctions in global politics. Indeed the *Prospect's* description and its visual support mesh together democracy, a political enterprise, with the heterosexual gaze, an apparatus of patriarchy. It seems safe, then, to argue that the heterosexual gaze, which constitutes what is and is not beautiful, maps out in readings of what a democracy can look like. Consequently, Benazir Bhutto as the self-consciously modern, Pakistani democratic heroine functions as a representation of democracy ensconced in dominion and domination.

In the foreground of this poster, we see a Pakistani women, lighting candles, grief-stricken. The juxtaposition of Bhutto as a powerful, glamorous woman leading Pakistan toward a democracy against the masses of Pakistani working and middle class wo/men allows us to visualize the wide range of Pakistani cultural structures while simultaneously using the bourgeois body to signify modernity, political desirability and the power of heterosexual aesthetics. The image of men and women grieving Bhutto functions as the media's (empty) gesture towards authenticity, an opportunity to imagine the Pakistani masses. But the vitality of the photograph lies in the *jouissance* of looking upon an *other* that is perfectly palatable to the west, and hence, grieved.

Public mourning, as we know, is not a spontaneous expression of grief but a symbolic and political practice. In keeping with the ethos of modern political grief, this visuality demonstrates a number of things. The visual techniques figure Bhutto as a heroic protagonist who deserved protection but did not receive it, while the masses bear the weight brought about by her assassination through the failure of the Pakistani or international institutions to intercede on Bhutto's behalf. The message is poignantly directed: *Bhutto should be alive: she could have saved Pakistan.* It is the interplay of the two parts of this photograph that grounds, filters and transmits the moral message of Bhutto as catastrophe and consumption of Pakistan. This picture is organized around the enormity of Pakistan's political strife even as it reduces its sheer size to one political heroic figure. This photograph finds ample ideological support in the asymmetrical theatre of witnessing that allows the west to view, read and comprehend the ruins of *othered* nations (Williams 2010; Žižek 2008)

One of the key goals of this chapter is to illustrate how language and visualities of Bhutto produce rather than reflect knowledge, subjectivity and regimes of democracy. First appearing in *The DailyMail*, a

Four. Is There a Queer Democracy? Or—Stop Looking Straight

British press, and reprinted in a number of venues from the *New York Times*, *BBC*, *The Washington Post*, *Daily Times*, and *Time* magazine, after her assassination; I want, now, to point to a popular image of Bhutto (*dailymail.uk*, 28 December 2007). The photograph is a double shot of Bhutto, a before and after shot of her entry into political life. On one side, we see Bhutto as college student—young, demure, her hair a touch disheveled, dressed in Western clothes, described as an "Oxford party girl" and "party throwing student." The picture is black and white. On the other side and in color, we see Bhutto as a woman, just inaugurated as prime minister of Pakistan. She is wearing a brown printed Pakistani tunic, and in what will become the quintessential Benazir look, a white *dupatta* loosely frames her face, covering her hair just slightly so that it still "gleams through" (Stan 2007). The heading of the article reads, "Benazir Bhutto: Oxford Party Girl Cursed by Blood Soaked Dynasty."

Laced with the contradictions of nation, class, and gender, these photographs allow us to see how Bhutto came to iconoclastically represent both Pakistan and the West, the imperial and the *other*, the local and the global, America's darling and Pakistan's daughter. Indeed, this visual rendering demonstrates the inescapable (Western) aestheticization of Bhutto in the global political theatre. Both photograph and text, here, reveal the subtle and schizophrenic investment in constructing an *other* that is at once *othered* and embraced, exotic and modern, erotic and Cartesian. The media that captured her (image) and brought her to (Western) spectators operates as a factory for the interpellation of subjects into ideology. Indeed, this photograph interpolates a hip, modern audience that comes to gaze at the feminine, racialized *other* as re-fashionable and re-definable in the Western cultural contexts. The aesthetic hierarchies through which Bhutto's democracy and leadership was projected foreclosed on potential understandings of Bhutto as colonized figure and Pakistani democratic formations as anything but Western tout court.

As a median destined to obtain precise ideological effect, the juxtaposition of the young "party girl" with an older, mature, coiffed, ethnically Pakistani Prime Minister Bhutto makes clear how subjectivity is read through specific feminine tropes. That Bhutto was more often not narrated through the tropes of Western hetero-erotics confronts the symbolic democracy that was articulated through her. As Boehmer (2005) argues, beauty functions as an index to democracy in the postcolonial field. The political utterance and its organizing visuality that places female national subjects as beautiful draws attention to the politics of a sexualized democracy that shapes the constitution of desirable feminine/feminist subjects and the ways this politics participates in the reproduction and enabling of empire. The *SATC2* scene, where the Muslim women's disrobing of the *niqab* reveals their liberation through the textuality of their couture body signs into the imperial gaze a phallocratic dimension, a fetishistic scopophillia that interrupts a liberatory democracy. *Time* magazine's photograph discussed earlier of the young Afghani woman's disfigured face as sound evidence for a democratizing war affirms this point as well. But, of course, Bhutto is a multidimensional political figure. She is neither a fictional, entertaining character nor an oppressed brown woman. Her presence in the modern world's political field implies a changing of the subject that has dominated national and imperial politics. But does it?

Benedict Anderson (1983) has spoken of particular kinds of texts as tightly associated with the compositions of nationalists' imaginations and movements. But I want to assign to Bhutto's textuality a very crucial place in the inscription of, not the Pakistani nation, but of empire. Portrayed as a powerful woman pushing against the often bleak portrayal of the feminine, racialized *other*, this supposition firmly rests on her upper-class status, her conciliatory relationship to the U.S., and her ability to usher Western sensibilities into Pakistan. As I've shown thus far, the dominant framing of Bhutto as symbolic of democracy occurred most poignantly through her visual and corporeal landscape. This invisible dialogue, or pact even, between democracy and the body is curious as it opens a space to interrogate the necessary conflation of hetero-erotics, white aesthetics, and Western democracy. Pierre Bourdieu's (1984) concept of *habitus* demonstrates that the values, attitudes and ideologies of society are literally embodied. Body size, clothes, aesthetics demeanor, ways of eating, sitting, speaking, and making gestures all reveal the social structures embedded in the body. Similarly, in *Discipline and Punish*, Foucault (1982) redefines the body as the site where political power is exercised. In the image of Bhutto's vigil, we see how American democracy, through its value-inculcating and value-imposing operation, helps to form a general, transposable disposition towards democratic culture and the inscription of the bourgeoisie (Bourdieu 1984).

The democratic leader is an object of admiration because she most efficiently and accurately reproduces mainstream cultural images of success, heterosexual aesthetics, hard work and glory and because she efficiently and in the most advanced manner represents culturally legitimate interests, lifestyles and successes. Her body is a topography saturated with elitist class.

Bhutto is produced as a subject of democracy who is not only intellectually outstanding but morally in tune,[3] aesthetically pleasing, and in touch with the value of femininity and heteronormativity. She is democratic not only because she believes in this political enterprise, but because she is the perfect complement to the "truth" of modernity and is eminently likable, hence faithful, to the west. The *American Prospect* (Stan 2007) substantiates this in the statement: "deftly wielding her Ivy League education, she had plenty of intelligence to accompany her beauty and charm, as well as an uncanny ability to synthesize the aspirations of her South Asian nation with the longings of its Western patrons." The equilibrium assumed between the aesthetic and the ethical, the modern feminine and democratic potentialities signify the relationship between symbolic freedom and the erotics of empire.

The conditions of entry into democracy marked by acquisition of tastes, manners, attitudes, desires and forms of leisure can be traced through the visual portrayals of Bhutto. Bhutto's symbolic mastery of Western life and aesthetics render her deeply palatable to the dominant gaze and infuse her with authority on the transmission of democracy (Bourdieu 1984). Democracy, citizenship, civility, productivity and high arts are ideologies that are by and large reproduced by and reflected in Western bourgeois lifestyles, concerns and epistemologies. Conceptually, democracy is presented as the opposite of bourgeois values, as a political ideal and practice that privileges participation, immanence, deliberation and inclusion (Dean 2009; Young 2000; Held 1995). But real, existing constitutional democracies privilege the wealthy as they install, extend, and protect neoliberal capitalism (Dean 2009; Held 1995). Bhutto, both linguistically and visually, illustrates a proclivity towards these ideologies. Her dress, style, self-responsibility, sexualized, feminine embodiment are inherently linked to classist notions of goodness and humanity, while her engagement of the political sphere, the language of democracy, and tropes of modernity are integrally connected to capitalist privilege.

Aesthetics in capitalist society function as a mechanism of power, of acquisition, not just of material wealth, but cultural belonging. Bourdieu (1984:76) writes:

> It is also a sense of belonging to a more polished, more polite, better policed world, a world which is justified in existing by its perfection, its harmony and beauty, a world that has produced Beethoven and Mozart and continues

Figure 5. Pakistan's former prime minister, Benazir Bhutto, gets ready for her last public rally in Rawalpindi, Pakistan, on December 27, 2007 (AP Photo/B.K. Bangash).

Four. Is There a Queer Democracy? Or—Stop Looking Straight

to produce people capable of playing and appreciating them. And finally it is an immediate adherence, at the deepest level of the habitus, to the tastes and distastes, sympathies and aversions, fantasies and phobias which, more than declared opinions, forge the unconscious unity of a class.

The message the media transmits, through Bhutto's photographic narrative, is a highly provocative and class saturated message. Aesthetics serves, either consciously or not, as a measure of how modern Bhutto can be. Discourses on aesthetics, and beauty specifically, are heavily associated with ideologies that reflect, encourage and reproduce class in highly bourgeois ways (Bordo 1997; Collingham 2001). These discourses continue to transform in problematic ways "necessities into strategies, constraints into preferences and ... generates the sets of choices constituting lifestyle" (Bourdieu 1984: 175). The status of Bhutto as democracy's political fantasy, then, has deeply social, symbolic, and libidinal mechanisms (Dean 2009).

To elaborate, let me bring another intriguing photograph (**see fig. 5**) to bear on this discussion. Here, we see Bhutto's profile, the white *dupatta* framing her hair, a red flower from the garland around her neck peeping through. With one hand she holds what looks like a small book to her face and with the other, she applies and adjusts red lip gloss. As stated by the *UK DailyMail*, "seconds before she takes the stage for her final rally, Bhutto is seen applying makeup" (*dailymail.co.uk*, 27 Dec 2007). Thirteen years earlier, during her stint as Prime Minister, a *New York Times* (15 May 1994) statement reaffirms this intrigue in her feminine aesthetics. The *Times* states, "Her red-lipsticked visage on an election poster offered a promise of modernity in a nation that suffered an inferiority complex next to its rival and motherland, India."

The metaphoric use of lipstick (or, lip gloss) to signify both beauty and modernity indeed substantiates Anzaldua's (1990: xv) striking point that "the face is the surface of the body that is the most noticeably inscribed by social structures, marked with instructions on how to be mujer, macho, working class, chicana." The framing of Bhutto as modern vis-à-vis her red lipstick or as aesthetically oriented vis-à-vis lipstick application before her (fatal) rally, however, raises a number of concerns. What Collingham (2001) calls the processes of Anglicization, where the brown Indian body in British colonial times was subtly transformed and reformatted to give off distinctly Anglo-Indian signifiers of Britishness, is a useful rendering here. The application of the red lip gloss metonymically functions to Westernize her, make her more familiar to constructions of Western femininity. But they also point to how the ideologies of aesthetics and prestige that ordained readings of Bhutto in the global political theatre bolstered the imperial formulas of racialized bodies gaining power through an embodiment of racial and class superiority.

The relentless representation of Bhutto's body and aesthetics as relevant to global readings of what democracy looks like is indeed troubling. These narrations of Bhutto locate American interest in her, not within the realms of her metonymical relationship to the life-worlds of the Pakistani people and political transitions of the Pakistani national government, but within the field of hetero-erotics wherein she articulates, through her body, the changing time and space of postcolonial Muslim nations, while holding in place the exotic aesthetics of femininity and ideological distance of the *other*. Moreover, the *Times* move to strategically posit a backward Pakistan (that can move forward) through an invocation of the feminine subject and body is an important, if not problematic, one. Rhetorically shaping Pakistan as insecure to its "rival" India and that these insecurities are ameliorated (or not) vis-a-vis particular feminine corporealities is a key dimension of imperial democracy, as Eisenstein (2007) and Enloe (2006) argue. The language used by the *Times* cements how Bhutto's appeal was expressed largely though the landscape of the (elite) female body and how Bhutto inspired a palatable Pakistan, one that could only be imagined through the landscape of her domesticated body. Grewal's (2005, 95) point that American concepts of democracy and women's liberation circulate transnationally, and that women and their chosen or unchosen representations "absorb, utilize and rework the notion of America into particular agendas and strategies within which their bodies play an uneven and heterogeneous role," is relevant here. Lipstick as a synecdoche for modernity, seems to render visible geopolitical insecurities, which, then, effectively instantiates a form of democracy that distinctively relies on and utilizes a hetero-erotic gaze.

Narrative, like metaphor, can be said to have discursive materiality; therefore the story of Bhutto permits the forging and testing of particular kinds of affiliations and loyalties. Bhutto's story is said to embody Pakistan. But in pointing to the tropes and devices through which her story came to be told and desired, I engage in a refusal to overlook the necessary conflation of Bhutto qua democracy and Bhutto qua beautiful. Instead, to the extent that Bhutto's story became virtually synonymous with notions like democracy, modernity, progress, and beauty, I depart from the sanctioned narrative of Bhutto as Pakistan, and instead locate her as empire's subject par excellence.

As chapters two and three have shown, in the U.S. imagination, the brown female subject enters into discussion only when she can critically function to evidence the barbarism of such nations, as we see in Mukhtar Mai, or if she serves in the popular mobilization of the construction of the New Woman, as is the case with Bhutto. Whereas Mai, dipped in the metaphoric surplus of the fantasy of brown oppression, came to signify national authenticity but one replete with precarity due to the kind of anti-patriarchal work within which she engaged, Bhutto's (white) aestheticized femininity secured her iconic status as democratic leader. The symbolic valence of democracy under which Bhutto became popularized conflates sexual politics with imperial geography. The slippery semantics and gaze directed at Bhutto taps into the varying ways pleasure and power produce particular cultural meanings over and through the female body. Whether Bhutto's visual and narrative subjectification is rooted in material facticity or a purely fictive invention, this storytelling in producing such a seductively powerful contemporary feminine figure relies on racist, classist and imperialist formulations of gazing at the *other.*

Benazir Bhutto's signification as a Pakistani, democratic, modern, desirable, public and feminine symbol is not fixed in advance. Once imagined, this "politician with the spellbinding looks of a 1940's movie star," comes to signify and symbolize these identities through narrative and nonnarrative metaphoric surplus (*New York Times*, 15 May 1994). By fixing Bhutto beneath the evaluative epithets "spellbinding looks" and "beauty and charm" the dominant narratives give way to its tendency to objectify women even as its grants them access to the global political theatre. Within the socio-symbolic field in which Bhutto came to be iconoclastic, descriptions of her oscillated between this fetishistic fascination with her beauty, a voyeurism rooted in *seeing* her (body and bodily practice) and the (un)easy exhibitionism of her political/cultural habitus. In Bhutto's projected image lived a meeting of east and west, and a glimpse at what a modern South Asia could be: cosmopolitan, erudite, stylish, and friendly to the west. Indeed, she had the smile down pat. The metaphorical meanings laced in the repertoire of Bhutto's images confirm an ideal love of the West, as a form of style, aesthetic and freedom. The creation of Bhutto as democratic icon is indeed one of the ideological implications of these set of photographs. Within this reading, Bhutto's gender was no impediment; it was, perhaps, her best accessory. Her very womanhood signaled a departure from the two main directors of Pakistani politics: the military and the mullahs, popularized by the 2003 *PBS* documentary on Pakistan titled, *The Rock Star and the Mullahs.*

Visual scholars have well established how photographs constitute a subject, often through the illusory delimitation of a central location (Sontag 2003: Baudry 1985). Images of Bhutto corroborate with a marked efficacy in the maintenance of political and (Western) feminine idealism. It is important to recognize that the construction and proliferation of Bhutto as heroine qua Pakistan is predicated upon figuring an individual that is palatable to the West. In order to function as a deserving heroine-victim, Bhutto's racial difference must be domesticated, a process visual and postcolonial scholars have often alluded to as central to the colonial and imperial fields (Bhabha 1996; Collingham 2001; Williams 2010). Bhutto's domesticated worthiness emanated from her ruling-class pedigree, from her *habitus*.

A *BBC* series, entitled a *Life in Photos: A Cursed Dynasty*, produced in December 2007 after her assassination, speak poignantly to the in/appropriation of Bhutto as a palatable subject. A set of 15 photographs trace the trajectory of Bhutto's political life, with the last of six photographs visually spelling out her final fatal rally and the uprisings after her assassination. These photographs speak provocatively to the anglicized aesthetic that shaped global readings of Bhutto as democratic symbol par excellence. Every image follows a set of telling aesthetic conventions. Some capture a younger Prime Minister Bhutto. The photographs focus on her face, black kohl lining her eyes, and red lipstick perfectly etched on her lips. She is sitting and her hand is raised and folded under her chin, propping her face upwards. Her face is chiseled and smooth. Her expression is serious and sober. We see her dark hair. A white *dupatta* loosely frames her face. Others capture her in her noticeably Western youth. These images tend to be black and white. The camera has caught her mid-laughter in her Oxford days, familiarly dressed, desirably engaged. In these photograph, Bhutto is a deeply familiar subject. Her posture, her dress, her affect effectively locate her in a Western *habitus*, a *habitus* that signifies more than class, alluding to white multiculturalism and white fantasy. In both, her aesthetics, her posture, her demeanor speak to a desirable, recognizable *habitus*.

Indeed, every image of Bhutto follows these aesthetic conventions, even the most recent ones of her entry into the Pakistani political scene. They are usually of Bhutto sitting on a sofa or speaking from behind a

Four. Is There a Queer Democracy? Or—Stop Looking Straight

podium. More often than not, the camera is angled downward from above her shoulder. Rarely do we see her full body. Her expression is almost always subdued but not daunting, not overly serious, but sober and pleasant. A white *dupatta* always loosely frames her face and often, we see an adornment or two, perhaps a ring on her finger or an earring shines out from under her hair. Black khol lines her eyes, which sometimes fully engage the camera and other times appear to dismiss the camera when it has caught her in action or in thought. While these photographs are meant to show us the most contemporary Bhutto, the Bhutto the American audience became privy to in a post–9/11 landscape; a Bhutto through whom the west began to imagine the possibilities of a democratic Pakistan, they relentlessly focus on her face, in ways that renders her palatable, desirable, and recognizable. She is wistful or smiling, or reflective, her hand is over mouth and she appears in deep thought. Her eyes are dark, her mouth red, her aesthetics largely anglicized, ethnicized only by the white *dupatta*, which doesn't disrupt her aesthetic in the way it apparently interrupts Mai's possible empowerment. Bhutto is positioned uniquely to this Pakistani feminine attire in that it doesn't upset her "modern" self-presentation. Instead, it authenticates her as the *real* Pakistani woman, but one that confirms Western aesthetics, bears out democracy despite resistance, and validates the desire to see Pakistan as palatable.

In this popular, globally circulated photo spread, Bhutto is ossified as a desirable *other*. So, while, thus far, I have located Bhutto on my axis of the feminine, racialized *other*, in a number of ways she was never constituted as the raced *other*. Frankly speaking, she wasn't the picture of what the west imagined as "brown"; in that she was lighter-skinned. From the taunts of early colonialism to the benevolence of the cult of empire, the sun-darkened skin, often seen as stained by outdoor manual work is the visible stigma of brownness (McClintock 1995; Said 1979). The vocabularies constructing Bhutto and the ways in which she was more often than not photographed were predicated on an anglicized body, one that that we see in **fig. 4**. The metaphor unfolding around Bhutto was predicated on a deeply classed, anglicized physical beauty, a phallocratic obsession with her as beautiful. With the burgeoning images of brown men as dangerous, alongside the growing vision of brown women as victims, Bhutto came to be intimately associated with an aesthetic Pakistan, a magically beautiful cleanser of a polluted country. Bhutto's light-skinned, bright-lipped representations served as a technology of

Pakistani purification, inextricably intertwined with the semiotics of empire's new racism as well as class denigration. This racist logic is what allows Bhutto to emerge beautifully as the quintessential compliant *other*. As a feminine/feminist subject, Bhutto lived and moved within the constraints of highly regulated gender schemas, but schemas that produced her as the paradigmatic Pakistani female leader, making intelligible the domain of livable, desirable bodies but also the domain of unthinkable, abject, unlivable bodies (read the female religious martyrs of the Red Mosque).

Let's turn to **figs. 5** and **6**. In both figures, we see an older, campaigning Bhutto from the 2007 Pakistani electoral politics. In both photographs, the camera has caught her in the midst of adjusting her *dupatta* to keep it from falling off. In a gesture well-known throughout Pakistan, this image of Bhutto adjusting her *dupatta* was one of the most common ways she was photographed. While many critics of Bhutto saw her donning of the *dupatta* as merely a social mask of her (inauthentic) Pakistani femininity, in 2007, when she reentered the political scene, Bhutto stated repeatedly that democracy shouldn't mean the sacrifice of the *dupatta* for women. This position by Bhutto coupled with the ideological effect of Bhutto adjusting her *dupatta* as she moves through masculinized political fields raises a number of anxieties around the Pakistani female body and its relationship to democracy. It seems wise to ask why the *dupatta*, an article of clothing, is held as paradoxical to democracy, a political system. Does democracy require an expungement of unfamiliar feminine tropes so much so that Bhutto must publicly reconcile one with the other?

I argue that Bhutto's *dupatta* functioned as an elusive play between fantasy, politics and desire. Her statement captures the antinomies of social difference, underscoring the ambivalence and incomplete character of modern identities or democratic processes as they actually are inhabited. Her desire to symbolically coalesce this dichotomy, the *dupatta* with democracy, dramatizes the significance of the female body to Western political enterprise. This dichotomy is a serious one. On the one hand, we know democratic subjectivity relies on Cartesian formulations of the modern political subject, which produce gender-neutral rather than a gender-embodied democracy. The action of the photographs fasten Bhutto's (however dubious) statement; hence, reorganizing the Cartesian nature of democracy while simultaneously placing both the woman subject and the female body in the tenuous contemporary

Four. Is There a Queer Democracy? Or—Stop Looking Straight

Figure 6. Benazir Bhutto speaks to the media at her headquarters in Karachi, Pakistan, on November 20, 2007 (AP Photo/Shakil Adil).

position of having to evidence that Islam and democracy were reconcilable.

As Susan Bordo (1993:143) makes clear, "women, besides *having* bodies, are also associated with the body, which has always been considered a woman's sphere in family life, in mythology, in scientific, philosophical and religious ideology." Hence, on the other hand, both image and rhetoric stress the hyper-relevance of the body, reproducing Descartes' dualistic axis of mind over matter, where the body functions as "a cage" or a "prison" (Augustine in Pine-Coffin 1961). If the rational self of the West is secured in its universal scope and authority by performing necessary exclusions of all that is bodily, feminine, emotional and intersubjective (Butler 1999; Grosz 1994), how, then, is Bhutto secured as desirable political subject to the west, within the constraining fields of race and gender?

The fantasy of democratization, in its most contemporary manifestations, relies on a particular kind of racialization and hetero-eroticism that allowed Bhutto to prevail as democratic célèbre. The brown female subject, whether one subjected to the human rights gaze or one awakened by U.S. democracy, is rendered desirable through the dual processes of anglicization and hetero-eroticization. Consequently, I argue, even her donning of the *dupatta*, a Pakistani headscarf that has long symbolized feminine modesty, became the perfect complement to her otherwise anglicized self. This becomes apparent in a caption offered by *American Prospect*:

> She wore it in an acutely stylized and regal manner always white, loose, flowing, perched far enough back on her head to accent her high cheekbones and gleaming dark hair. It said, "I am woman." It said, "I am timeless" [Adele Stan, 2007].

What is this obsession with Bhutto's body or more largely, with these markers of orientalist femininity, the aesthetics of the female body and the woman subject? The *Prospect's* description of Bhutto locates Bhutto in Bourdieu's category of the "effortlessly elegant," as an embodiment of cultural capital by right of birth. But it is not so seamless. As a Pakistani woman, in spite of her class and political position, she falls also into the realm of subjects that need to be trained in the reproduction of aesthetic and cultural excellence. If, as Irigiray (1985) suggests, women stage femininity as an ironic performance, Bhutto's necessary masquerade of the *dupatta* and the fantasizing spectacle of her *dupatta* begs the integration of the female body as a vital element in (inter)national racist discourse, both on a symbolic and pragmatic level.

The language used to describe her donning of the *dupatta* functions to make this (foreign) practice palatable, desirable and, indeed, erotic. That her *dupatta* was "acutely stylized and regal" and "perched far enough back on her head to accent her high cheekbones and gleaming dark hair" keeps Bhutto, as a feminine, racialized *other*, both aesthetic and visible. In fact, the language literally shifts her subject positioning from an *other* who covers her hair to a stylized, recognizable subject. With her "high cheekbones and gleaming hair," Bhutto comes to be rhetorically rearranged in ways that create political subjectivity without the sacrifice of feminine desirability nor the erasure of colonial constructions of the mystic orient. The language imposed upon Bhutto suggests a metaideological operation: an epistemic operation that presses against the conscious to interfere with both her racialized and sexualized positioning in public space. Indeed, it is remarkable that the *dupatta* in Mai's case is seen as an impediment to her empowerment while in Bhutto's case the *dupatta* is utterly decontextualized and reoriented to timeless womanhood. The logic of hetero-democracy is that the *other* is welcomed "in" vis-a-vis their ability to rearrange their feminine, racialized "selves."

Recalling again the veiled women from the *SATC2* scene, we see how their "selves" were welcomed "in," deemed desirable and identifiable only after they dropped their *niqabs* to reveal their couture attire. Prior to that, there was neither pleasure (e.g., laughter) or security (e.g., there was palpable fear and trepidation in the foursomes' eyes). In this way, the semiotic inclusion of racial others is carefully evacuated of any undomesticated difference, such as unfamiliar aesthetic tropes (read veil) as well as critical voice and agency (read they just want to be like "us"). Grewal (2005) argues that central to discourses on Americanism was the narrative of progress and freedom within a framework of American exceptionalism, wherein the embodiment of an "American way of life" could exist inside and outside of the borders of American nation-state. What must be noted in her statement is that American-ness as a uniquely global concept allows for a shifting and changing national subject, a heterogeneity that still explicitly exhibits the fundamental tenets of a liberated, democratic subjectivity, a subject we see embodied by Bhutto. This form of racist democracy holds practical function as democratic identity depends not on whether the *other* has free "choice" but on whether the *other* makes "choices" similar to ours (Žižek 2008; Butler 2004).

Will the Real Pakistani Woman Please Stand Up?

Bhutto's statement on the *dupatta* and the press's statement on her *dupatta* rely on an empire whose racist and sexist character, as James Clifford (1988) has reminded, "allows us to say *this* about *that*." As a racist overture, this narrativization essentially creates that which is identifiable as undesirable, i.e., the foreigner, Islamist, and terrorist, to the floating identity, those *other* figures who are identifiable, intelligible, desirable. Hence, in the logic of the U.S. press, we see empire's double speak: in the invocation of universal beauty, global civil society, human rights, and democracy is the correlate obligation to be identifiable at all times, to keep oneself visible, aesthetic, modern and desirable before the state. The obvious inverse here is the field of veiled women (invisible subjects to, say, the French state[4]), masked terrorists who take actions against states, and of course, the veiled women martyrs of the Pakistani state, whom I discuss in chapter five.

Within these neoformations of racialization, which rely on women's hypervisibility, democracy is nothing more than a vacuous term, holding no meaning because it is not a fixed standard of judgment but a qualifier whose meaning is fixed in relation to something else. Democracy becomes fashioned into a commodity, or something on a woman's body, that can be exported, sold to, or staged for consumption by the United States (Wallerstein 1983; Dean 2009). As democracy is granted primarily through these framings of Bhutto, "democracy" loses whatever substantive meaning it may have and becomes confined to the insidious hetero-erotic corporealities that seem to exercise it. It comes to operate as an axis that work towards reconceptualization of gender/race/class hegemony and inter/national hierarchies, inversely welcoming its accompanying objectification and fetishization.

The feminine ideal takes shape and thus finds its reflection in a political ideal that, under the sign of democracy, combines U.S. American imperial interest and the movement toward Pakistani sovereignty. But this feminine ideal, as we know historically from writers such as Bordo (1995) and Irigiray (1985) engenders a deeply sexual gaze. Bhutto was consistently read through her body even as there existed a total denial around her as an erotic subject. Insofar as all these descriptions of Bhutto depend on the female body and its normalized conventions and aesthetics, we see how this discursive gesture writes hetero-erotic aesthetics into key readings of democracy.

Benazir Bhutto is surely the most startling and striking illustration of how cavalier power relations are with respect to representing power-

Four. Is There a Queer Democracy? Or—Stop Looking Straight

ful, feminine, racialized *others*. Yet she is also the canvas on which we come to see how deeply these power relations are etched on female bodies and how well these bodies serve them in a number of ways, ways that Mai resisted and the Red Mosque martyrs eschew all together. In many ways, Bhutto's constant reduction to her aesthetic practices and body can be paralleled in readings of American female political leaders such as Hillary Clinton or Sarah Palin, where they are varyingly reduced to feminine tropes of sexual objectification, as either pathologically desexualized or fetishistically hyper-sexualized as America's sex kitten. Clinton, specifically framed as a "castrating" public figure (Koehler 2011) was in the odd position of having to prove that she's tender enough within an American political terrain where women usually have to prove they're tough enough (Rowland 2002). Indeed as recent as May 2011, Clinton crudely came to be embodied in things such as nutcrackers (Koehler 2011). Ironically, no similar discourse was at stake in the American political investment in Bhutto.

Doesn't it seem relevant to ask why Bhutto's gender was not emphasized in this all too familiar narrative as she stood to preside over "the most dangerous place on earth?" What ideological contours can be traced in the American political interest in Bhutto as President of Pakistan when her desirability within Western political discourse relied not on her machismo, but dwelled on her femininity? Bhutto had to prove that she was tough enough to collaborate with the Pakistani army (Musharraf) and take on the Taliban. But representations of Bhutto suggest that the safety (and desire) found in her was, indeed, palimpsestic, containing many layers of American desire, Western security and Pakistani (male) servitude. The feminine excesses of Bhutto's aesthetics served a distinct and critical function in reference to the war on terror.

It is crucial to note that Bhutto, as feminist and democratic célèbre, did not flourish when imperial ebullience was at its peak. She emerged during an era of impending Pakistani crisis and international terrorist calamities, serving to preserve, through feminine fetish ritual, the uncertain boundaries of class, gender and race identity in a social order felt to be threatened by the fetishistic effluvia of (male) terrorism, anti–American sentiments, imperial competition and anti-colonial resistance. Bhutto offered the promise of imperial regeneration through the landscape of her modern femininity, restoring the threatened potency of the imperial body politic and the white(r) race. But her visualities also disclose a crucial paradox. On one hand, Bhutto embodied the hope of empire's progress, as she articulated a pro–American stance. At the same time, Bhutto's popularity in the Pakistani political scene, despite allegations of financial corruption and disdain for her husband, also complicates the gaze that cast Pakistan as a tight, unyielding patriarchy. Her popularity raises new questions about the relationship between Pakistani national discourse and female political figures, pointing to the deliberate unevenness of definitive patriarchies.

Contemporary metaphorizations that followed Bhutto's political rhetoric and self-presentation are so amorphous that they tend to repudiate any locality for cultural thickness, yet they spoke lucidly to Pakistan's contemporary repositioning in the global context. The figure of Bhutto tends to function in a very specific way as the embodiment of modernity, financial capital, anti-terrorism, pro–American and so on. Indeed, she locates herself in this function. The fall 2009 issue *Parade*, an American popular culture magazine, offers another compelling narrative (http://www.usatoday.com/search/Parade%20Magazine/). In this image, we see Bhutto's classic public face. She is wearing a white *dupatta* loosely over her head so we still see her dark hair. Red lipstick, what the Pervez Sharma (2011) of *Huffington Post* calls her "signature bright lipstick," covers her lips as they spread in a quintessential Bhutto expression. It is neither a smile nor a frown. It is a look of pleasantness, but strong, interested yet aloof. Her eyes appear softer than her mouth. To the side of this photo are the words, "I am what the terrorists fear the most—a female political leader fighting to bring modernity to Pakistan. Now they're trying to kill me" (*Parade* Magazine, Fall 2009, "An Interview with Gail Sheehy").

In Bhutto, we see nothing but the desire to modernize Pakistan, a modernity that occurs largely through a marriage of neoliberalism and democracy (Dean 2009). As a number of scholars have articulated, in Pakistan, modernity and the multiplicity of processes and manifestations associated with it sits on an ambivalent terrain invoking legitimacy and desirability simultaneous to inciting an urgent antagonism with the current state of affairs (Rashid 2006, Jamal 2004). The words accompanying this photograph show that imperial modernity is not shaped around a single privileged category, such as democracy (Dean 2009). Instead, the formative categories of imperial modernity—race, class, gender, sexuality, nation—are articulated in and through each other in dynamic, shifting and intimate interdependencies. The ideological charge of Bhutto as (Pakistani) nation functions, in effect, to justify the rearrangement of her privilege and authority in situating Pakistan as a player in the modern

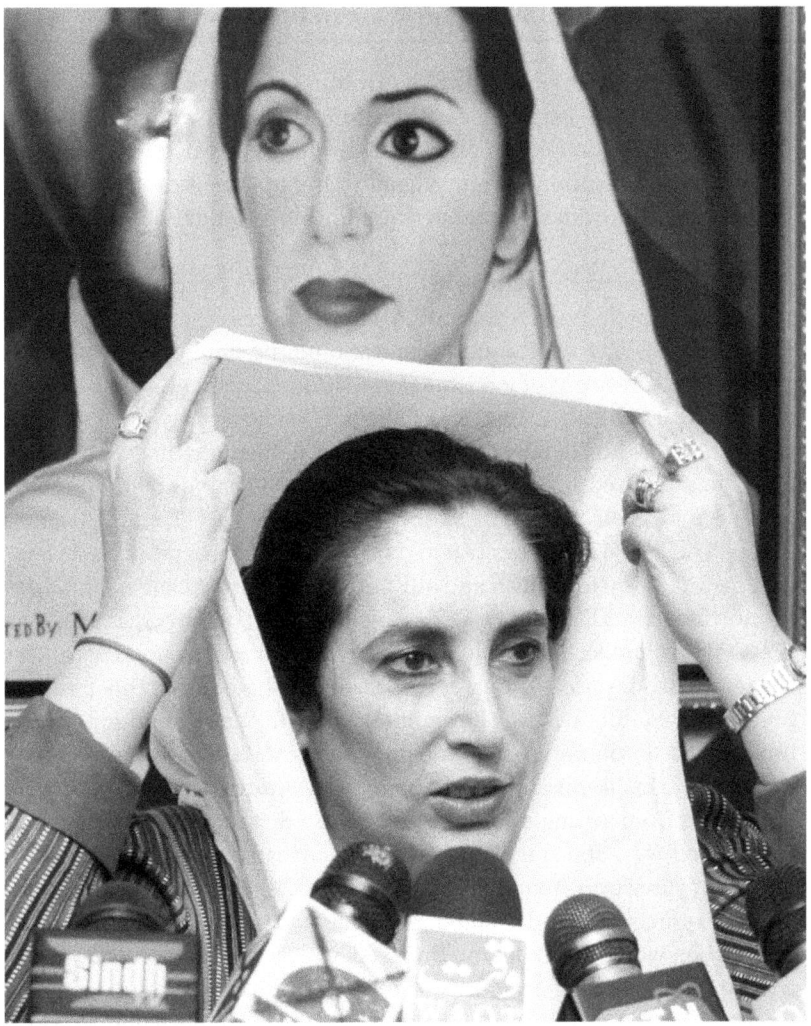

Figure 7. Pakistan's former prime minister, Benazir Bhutto, adjusts her scarf during a news conference in Karachi, Pakistan, on November 27, 2007 (AP Photo/Fareed Khan).

world. The narrative of Bhutto as democratic subject par excellence in the throes of terrorist danger and death cashes in on a narrative currency that rigorously polices women's bodies and sexualities in order to read them as modern or not. Bhutto's gender rituals and her Western aesthetic merge here to overdetermine her as the symbol of what the terrorists most fear. Bhutto is cast as without (Islamic) ideology, performing politics in the service of the global economy, avoiding any hint of critical agency. The potentially disrupting or disturbing facts of woman-ness and Pakistani-ness which might otherwise disqualify Bhutto from her meritorious heroinification, is neutralized in her apparent desire to accept Pakistan as subordinate to America and, more broadly, in the global economy.

But, of course, this narrative of heroics is inversely gendered, where (brown) masculinity is yet again charted as excessive, dangerous, and untrustworthy. Let us, for example, examine the implications of juxtaposing then-President of Pakistan, Pervez Musharraf to Benazir Bhutto. Musharraf was oft described as a Pakistani leader who "wore a western suit and tie," who "liked dogs" (something named anathema to Islam) and who possessed an "ease with Western ways" (*The National* 18 August 2008, *Hindustani Times* 11 October 2005, *New York Times* 7 January 2007). The *New York Times* (Ajami 2007) sums Musharraf up in its caption: "a dictator with charm and guile and a modernist veneer who rules exotic, dangerous lands." These seemingly absurd contours that allow the West to trace modernity through subjective social and corporal behaviors suggest that, despite shifting readings of Musharraf over his political tenure, he, like Bhutto, was brought in line with Western notions of the unique and autonomous individual. What's interesting to note is how differently Musharraf is photographed than Bhutto. He was often photographed from an angle of reverence or at a distance in a largely unromanticized way, and the camera was less invested in fragmenting him or his body in ways often seen in Bhutto's photographic displays. Certain photographic styles and techniques are linked to objectification. Most often when women's bodies are involved, the photographs are shot from a closer angle, honing in on aspects of face or body or clothing, cutting off a piece of time and space, allowing the viewer to relish and fixate on its object. Hence, both Musharraf and Bhutto personified the autonomous individual that human rights produces as subject par excellence—a citizen endowed with rights, Aristotle's speaking political being,[5] and self-consciously modern wo/man.

However, despite this remarkable accomplishment, Musharraf was still located within imperial machinery that could only conjure the brown man as the dangerous *other* or the surreptitious greedy *other* (Bhattacharya 2008; Puar 2007; Jarmakani 2008). The male political figure, unlike Bhutto, functions in the imperial imagination as one of moral liminality, as one distinctly linked to the excessive patriarchies of Pakistan

Four. Is There a Queer Democracy? Or—Stop Looking Straight

and Islam. The imperial gaze which constitutes itself as the liberator of the Muslim woman is masked by the feminine, light skin of Bhutto, whose symbiotic authenticity (and an assassination presumably by Taliban members although there are a number of conspiracy theories abound) renders truthful this perception.

Bhutto is all smiles, wit, grace, and fashion: Musharraf is plodding, industrious, sober and precise. Such a reading is, of course, based on ideologies around brown men as menaces as opposed to Bhutto's visual seductiveness, where both readings have no real presence in Pakistani reality. As we know, ideology sustains, at the level of fantasy, precisely what it seeks to avoid at the level of actuality. So ideology appears to involve both sustenance of (particular) bodies and avoidance of *othered* bodies (Žižek 2008). Indeed, framing Bhutto as the missing piece in a Pakistani political puzzle dominated by mullahs and the military successfully lures the spectator into a political aesthetic that is both successfully redolent of a vanishing orientalist nostalgia but controllable. Bhutto comes to represent the *other* over whom there is complete mastery.

When prompted by *CNN's* Wolf Blitzer (2007), Bhutto said of Pakistan's Islamist groups, "[T]hey don't believe in women governing nations, so they will try to plot against me, but these are risks that must be taken. I'm prepared to take them." Similarly, in 2007, Bhutto stated for *The Economist*, "Pakistan is under severe threat of being taken over by extremists. This is why I feel it is essential to save Pakistan through democracy." Bhutto's words here spell out the economics of the imperial gaze, where she becomes both complicit in reestablishing the hierarchy of America over Pakistan, west over east, even as she defies the gaze that pigeonholes Pakistani women as weaker (or more oppressed) than their male counterparts. Her above statements blur the lines between Pakistan's patriarchy and imperial patriarchy, drawing directly from the former in order to render the latter invisible and deniable.

Despite the fact that many non-Islamic groups were also not happy with Bhutto, Bhutto called on those who opposed her fundamentalist and she was loved in the west for this and by many members of the Pakistani elites. The Western media bought this line because they saw Bhutto as the exotic woman who was deserving of power. For the elites and those who control the army, control of the nation is a class issue they do not want to share power and resources with the lower class and so the same justification applies, control of the lower class who are called fundamentalists (when we bomb villages in the North and in Baluchistan we tell ourselves are bombing extremists and fundamentalists). And yes, those who challenge the dominant groups in Pakistan do use the language of religion to articulate their demands. In this, they draw upon the message of Islam, which is fundamentally about justice (although women might take issues with some parts of this message). But it is important to note here that the religious parties are the least controlled by the landed gentry and the upper classes.

As such, Bhutto presents a spectacular textual event that the imperial camera fantasizes about and indeed, develops a monopoly over. Positing her at the intersection of two worlds, coagulating race, nation, class and gender into seamless aesthetic spectacles, the camera and accompanying rhetoric constitute Bhutto as an erotic national heroine. The spectacle of Bhutto controlling Pakistan's political terrain is actually a voyeuristic substitute for the psychological reinforcement of a Pakistan that needs to be tamed. By strategically projecting violence and sexual excess onto the brown male *other*, the dominant gaze constitutes the brown man as the repository of sexual and gender excess. Bhutto, however, translated and explained Pakistan as a trainable political object whose cultural, temporal and geographical distance and male citizenry were expressed in metaphors of danger, secrecy and deceit. Bhutto functions as the perfect foil to them, as she then seamlessly sanitizes the hyper-masculinized/nationalized space with her aesthetically femininized and modern self (Gopinath 2005; Puar 2007). From *Sex and the City 2's* trading in banal, unsophisticated orientalist fantasies to Bhutto's syntax on Pakistani men, we see how anti–Muslim propagation is becoming the most expeditious passage to national belonging.

Frantz Fanon (1963) observed how the national bourgeoisie—fundamentally an ethnicized middle-class with access to the colonizer's resources—was needed for the success of colonizing politics. Recall in my discussion of *SATC2's* book club scene, I argued that identity formation draws upon the image of the *other*, allowing for an affirmation of (white, Western) self. Bhutto's visuality is the seductive repository of the west's most tenacious and precarious self-idealization. Bhutto's politicized visual imagery creates such a strong sense of subjectivity in the spectator (of that image) that all other subjectivities (through which to reimagine that image of Bhutto) are thoroughly drained. By making the colonized *other* palatable in a certain way, the public unconscious could also be manipulated, the chaos of the nation domesticated, the racial-

Four. Is There a Queer Democracy? Or—Stop Looking Straight

ization of the *other* secured and upheld. As we know, democratic societies rely not on force but on propaganda, engineering consent by necessary illusion and emotionally potent oversimplification (Chomsky 2003; Dean 2009).

These potent oversimplification and visual illusions become even more apparent in the recently released documentary on Benazir Bhutto. Premiering at the 2010 Sundance Film Festival, in the tradition of documentaries, was *Benazir Bhutto: The Film* (http://www.bhuttofilm.com), produced by Duane Baughman. The cover, advertising the film, reads: "DEMOCRACY IS THE BEST REVENGE." The trailer runs like this: "From one of the most dangerous places on earth, in a land where women didn't matter, comes the story of a woman who had the courage to accept her destiny." These phrases come intermittently, in between vacillating images of jeeps filled with brown men holding large guns, women in *niqabs* with downcast eyes, shadowed foreboding mosques, fleeting images of past and present Pakistani dictators surrounded by a posse of men, and then Bhutto, young and stylish, eloquently speaking English as she moves through the masculinized spaces of Pakistani politics, claiming that the "regime couldn't touch her." The trailer literally fades off with these bold words—"martyr, accused, savior, scandal, charismatic, arrogant, courageous, controversial, legendary, and daughter"—each word accompanied by an image of Bhutto's lipsticked face, eyes, sunglasses, hair, raised arm, etc.

The film, itself, however, is more measured than the explosive trailer. It operates as an informational history of Pakistan's formation, its political seesawing between democratic and military regimes, and the role of the Bhutto family dynasty. While there is a definite romanticization of both Zulfiqar Ali Bhutto and Benazir Bhutto as stellar democratic figures through whom Pakistan experienced both stability and modernity, the general tone of the documentary is functional rather than sensational. Moreover, while the film critically lays out the ills of the U.S. in allowing for the proliferation of Islamist radical groups, it does overarchingly frame U.S. presence and intrigue in Pakistan as benevolent. For example, while the documentary acknowledges that the U.S.'s abandonment of Afghanistan after the Cold War led to the Islamic resurgency that Pakistan now experiences, it largely posits this abandonment as innocent. As the British narrator states in a reference to September 11, 2001, "it didn't occur to the U.S. that post–Cold War despair would sow the seeds for events two decades later." The discursive environment of the film supports American exceptional interest in Bhutto just as it also engages in a reservoir of terms and phrases that maintain the sanctity of this exceptionalism. Moreover, while the film only ambiguously locates Pakistan on Bush's "axis of evil," the viewer leaves the film, primarily but not only, having witnessed the excesses of (brown) colonial violence, despair, rage, and despotism. Hence the function of Bhutto's story, through the film, is to locate her outside of this and in the annals of democracy, modernity and Western aesthetics. Described in the film as both an "enrapturing woman" and "daughter of Pakistan" this cinematic representation posthumously continues the semantic traditions under which Bhutto came to be constructed as the desirable *other*. In fact, the producer of this film, Daune Baughman, when asked by *Huffington Post* journalist, Karen Badt (2010), why he made this film on Bhutto, says, "I've always been fascinated with Benazir Bhutto, how the images of Pakistan—the situation of women, the freedom of expression—are contradicted by the fact that they had a woman, a beautiful woman, a movie star woman, leading it, since 1988."

The transmutation of Pakistan's labyrinthine political history into the lesson of Bhutto speaks to the modernist ethos that locates democracy and women's rights firmly on the shoulders of the west, as at the least, the west can tell the story of the (unsavable) east. The symbolic capacity of a feminine, racialized political *other*, especially one whose racialization is domesticated by white aesthetics, to represent the perfectionist illusions of interventionary political action at a time when Islamic nationalism threatened the whole of Western culture reveals the specific utility of the discursive frames within which Bhutto came to symbolize democracy. As I argued in chapter two, using Mukhtar Mai and other brown visual subjects of human rights, humanitarian missions rely on images of domestic alterity (ideals of erotic domestication). The political imperative of making visible the (exceptional) *otherness* within which Bhutto's film operates is achieved at the cost of continually reanimating the ideological structures of legitimization that provide a convenient cover for the interventionary designs of new paranoid imperialism (Williams 2010). As R.W. Connell (1995) clarifies, the state is much more complicated than being governed by those who are identified as men or masculine. In hyper-aestheticizing Bhutto simultaneous to over-politicizing her national legacy to democracy (vis-à-vis her martyred father); empire cements its virility and pride even as it appears to emanate the empowerment of women. The stylized narratives on Bhutto's well-done femi-

Four. Is There a Queer Democracy? Or—Stop Looking Straight

ninity, her desirable aesthetics, and her sexual conduct came to represent quite crucially the rationalization for a new Pakistan, but a Pakistan that teetered on striking that perfect balance between Cartesian politics and embodied democracy.

What is carefully expunged from the trailer and the film are the contradictory traces that reveal the production and reproduction of postcolonial violence. The narrative and theatrical techniques deployed carefully deflect the power relations of north/south divide, engaging an imperialist historical amnesia around what generates violence and rage in the colony. The cultural scripts through which violence is viewed outside of the west are sanctioned in this cinematic display of Bhutto whose people couldn't keep her alive. Slavoj Žižek (2008:114) has argued, that "all politics relies upon, and even manipulates, a certain level of economy of enjoyment." In this regard, Bhutto's visual story is conceived and anticipated as metaphor and myth, as power and pleasure, as real and unreal. The political stakes in Bhutto's visuality are made readily apparent. The violent and incongruous juxtaposition of Bhutto as aesthetically and politically pure (read: "a woman who had the courage to accept her destiny") versus the reminder of Pakistan as always and already barbaric and misogynistic (read: "in a land where women didn't matter") depends on the deeply specific technologies of all these bodily displays, the veiled women, the gun-toting men, the suited politicians and then, Bhutto. The film both freezes her as spectacle and moves through her contradictory embodiment as fetish. As fetish, Bhutto and her body are effectively reorganized to embody her own status, to visually organize a singularity around democracy, hence women's freedom, in ways that became both carnivelesque and crudely naturalistic.

The final image caught of Bhutto seconds before her death, which circulated in newspapers and magazines throughout the Western world, elaborates this point (see, www.bbc.com, 2007, "In Pictures: Bhutto's Last Rally," http://news.bbc.co.uk/2/hi/in_pictures/7161751.stm). All conventions are in place—the red lipstick, white *dupatta* loosely framing her hair, her hand raised to adjust it from falling to the nape of her neck. This photograph portrays Bhutto as happy, ecstatic even. A generous smile spreads across her lips, her mouth slightly open in what looks like laughter. There is brightness in her eyes, as she stands upright into the sunroof of her bulletproof vehicle, wearing flowers around her neck and bangles on her hands. She is quintessentially Pakistani, elite, feminine.

In its exclusive focus on the victim-heroine and the failure of the

Pakistani government to save her, these photographs encode the dense materiality of violent history into a master narrative of virtual witnessing. On one hand, the images affirm the impossibility for an enlightened future in Pakistan, one accomplished through Bhutto. On the other hand, the axis of democracy shifts to the axis of spectacle, where the possibility of democracy in Pakistan is always and already dead by culture. The footage of Benazir Bhutto's death was played ad nauseum—is this not evidence of the carnivalesque character of democracy's liquidation? Indeed the axis of democracy is revealed here to be embedded in the conventions of spectacle.

The transmutation of the American imperial intervention in Pakistan into the testimonial of a failed state (one that annihilates its democratic figures, especially if they're female) is the emplotted product of the repeated footage of Bhutto's death. Like *Time* magazine's image and Mukhtar Mai's most widely distributed photograph, what is particularly aggressive about this final image is that in all its anticipatory horridness and (predicted) goriness, there lies a challenging kind of beauty, the sublime, an awesome or tragic register of the beautiful. So while Mai's post-rape image invoked a sublimity on the feminine, racialized oppressed *other*, this final photograph of Bhutto registers a spectacular parody of democracy because the viewer knows what happened after.

The final shot of Bhutto right before her assassination, is but one of several shots that necessarily spectacularized her death. The exhibitionism with which Bhutto's body was offered to her world viewers as textualized spectacle marginalizes what actually happened to Bhutto; the reality of her assassination remains lost in a web of conspiracy theories. History is reduced to a traumatic historical event—singular and archaized—to be consumed elsewhere as an entertaining injunction of "not again." That Pakistan has suffered cyclical problems of governance stemming from a weak political culture and an overdeveloped state (basically fuedalistic in its original and present construction) together with several economic distortions, numerous ideological dissensions and regional challenges remain marginalized.[6] Meanwhile, the voyeuristic spectacle of Pakistan's overall political and economic situation is successfully portrayed as dispiriting, confusing, and barbaric. While it is not the purpose of this chapter to attempt to discuss the labyrinthine and deeply controversial history of Bhutto's political trajectory, it seems a fair assessment to locate her fate within an epistemological framework through which Pakistan could be imagined and empire could be acted out. As such, through the screened consumption of Bhutto's death, the global mission of America is reanimated, secured and sanctified.

The spectacle of her death is indeed a celebrated instance of how dramatic nationalism and learned democracy come together in Said's (1979:78) "Orientalist theatre." The idea of repeatedly representing her death is a theatrical one: she is the stage on which the whole of Pakistan is imagined. Pakistan seems to be not a field in and of itself, but a theatrical stage affixed to America. In the depth of this stage, all my visual subjects nourish the American imagination. Bhutto, however, strategically operates as a figure whose outline needs to be sharpened to press ideological myths into the service of an advancing empire. Her visual subjectivity constitutes the power of feminine embodiment and heteroerotic aesthetics as specifically promulgated by contemporary processes of democraticization.

Queer Democracy or Straight Power: (Mis)Uses of the Female Body

In her essay, titled, "Is there a Queer Pedagogy? Or Stop Reading Straight," Deborah Britzman (1995) asks us to rethink the constitution of bodies of knowledge and knowledge of bodies within educational spaces, particularly as they organize perceptions of the gay and lesbian *other*. Through an exegetic discussion around the "unthought" in education, Britzman unsettles the sediments of what the dominant gaze imagines as normalcy and difference, empowerment and subordination, bodies of knowledge we compel and knowledge of bodies we impel. Tracing out the contours of ignorance that shape hegemonic reading practices, Britzman refuses the unassailability of *otherness* and the exorbitant normality of sameness. She compels a queer imagination around subjectivity, and hence, freedom of those subjects, that moves beyond voyeurism, spectatorship, and the materiality of the presence. In other words, she asks her reader to look beyond liberal tropes of inclusion, rights, voice and visibility to more radical imaginations on the free subject.

In invoking Britzman's (1995) title to frame my discussion of Bhutto, I too, render unstable the reading practices of democracy where the grounds of (empowered) identities are still confined to the mastery of

(Western) aesthetics and intelligibility. In reading Bhutto's visualities within the discourse of imperial hetero-erotics, I point to the misrecognitions, silences and ignorances embedded in straight democracies. To work within the terms of critical feminist, postcolonial, and queer theories, I've attempted in this chapter to think through the structures of disavowal within democracy that produce the feminine, racialized *other* as desirable or disruptive through a straight reading of her body.

The influx of Bhutto's imagery in the global political arena was said to have a significant effect on gender, destabilizing the media and political configurations that render women invisible or only visible as sex objects, if only because it makes us aware of how very rare it is to see a woman political leader. But depictions of Bhutto as exotic and erotic (in contrast to the destitute brownness of Pakistani *reality*) disrupt the possibilities of a politicized feminist and racialized self at which Bhutto's figure occasionally hints. In becoming American political spectacle, Bhutto bypasses a mode of subaltern and/or feminist compassion and, in ways too similar to Fanon's (1963) national bourgeoisie, she appears to take white society as the standard of measurement. The spectacle of Bhutto's female body "dusted over with colonial culture" (Fanon 1963) as representative of Pakistani, and more broadly, global democracy conceals the contestations and cross-linkages between the popular visual realm that relies on the white gaze and the subaltern imaginary that traverses the uneven and unstable framings of racialized political *others*.

My point here is not in Bhutto's collusion in the imperial economy and white aesthetics. That Bhutto had power that the other subjects I discuss didn't have access to catalyzes feminists' demands towards her, one which is superimposed on her and one I feel she navigated to disappointing ends. I do think Bhutto was strategically privileged to open up possibilities for redefining Pakistani women. For example, in Beijing, at the 1999 United Nations Fourth World Conference on Women, Bhutto was a key speaker advocating for the empowerment of women through education, employment and population control. She railed against female infanticide and misogynist interpretations of Islam (Khan 2007). Her presentation here is as a liberal humanist universal subject equally participating in a society that advocates an equality supposedly abstracted from race and gender, even as it relies on a classed aesthetic appearance. Bhutto's feminism was glorified only as it successfully effaced the radical praxis of feminist activists' lives, relied on the normalizing power of her imagery, incited a *jouissance* in her corporeal aesthetic and rendered

Four. Is There a Queer Democracy? Or—Stop Looking Straight

invisible the continued global north/south realities of domination and subordination.

When she transforms silence into voice, a woman transgresses, says Gloria Anzaldua (1995: xxii). But Anzaldua, even as she invokes this liberal trope, demands more of her feminist sisters and says, we have to choose with which voice and in which voice do we speak. Fanon tells us that being colonized by a language has larger implications for one's consciousness: "To speak ... means above all to assume a culture, to support the weight of a civilization" (1963:1718). Fanon elaborates by stating that speaking French means that one accepts, or is coerced into accepting, the collective consciousness of the French, which identifies blackness with evil and sin. Bhutto's ideological articulations at the Beijing conference, and throughout her post–9/11 political trajectory, proceeded from irreducible moral frameworks, such as democracy, human rights and modernity; hence, they impatiently foreclosed on the complexities of politics, the power embedded in representation and the imperial histories of her own specific context. Both democracy and feminism, if conceived through the spectacle of Bhutto, are imagined only in these specific and strategic visual terms, through the lens of imperial hetero-erotics.

Bhutto's discursive symbolization teeters ambivalently for and against configurations of power. In addressing the internal misogyny of the Muslim world, Bhutto remains unsatisfying to critical, postcolonial feminist callings. In speaking most fluently the language and logic of liberal, humanist frameworks, Bhutto attempts to escape the association of the feminine racialized *other* with oppression. Hence, it is not an exaggeration to say that rewriting Pakistani women's relationship to radical feminist work through a rewriting of Bhutto is an extension of the struggle between the feminist subaltern and the political elite. The seductive enterprise of female political visibility works within depoliticized democratic frameworks, perhaps what Žižek (2008) and Ranciere (2013) call post politics, where singular figures of resistance are allowed visibility within the deeply liberal-humanist and pleasurably cathartic frame of individual heroism and Pakistani failure. Fundamentally, then, no discursive destabilization occurred through Bhutto as, on the one hand, she was sandwiched between imperial motives, colonial wounds, national politics, the hetero-patriarchal state and cultural systems, and on the other, she reaped the benefits of each of these exploitive enterprises.

So while, through Bhutto, gender appears more nimble; she perhaps functions as Eistenstein's (2007) sexual decoy, where she brings into being the illusion of the power of political participation and the pleasure of freedom. By highlighting the ways Bhutto's visual aestheticization collided with nodes of power that use women's bodies to interpret freedom, oppression and global south/north relations, I wish to stress that most, if not all, relations between domination and subordination remain intact. Just as the gendered subject cannot escape the matrix of relationships and repetitions by which she is acculturated, she cannot become a perfect copy of the abstract woman, a perfect template for law that governs body and its performance of identity. Neither can the repetition and rituals of an aesthetic democracy create a perfect citizen.

In her essay on the struggle for progressive pedagogy, Walkerdine (1997:21) asks "at what costs this fantasy of liberation?" Similarly, in engaging the *hetero-erotic* "structures of intelligibility," to use Foucault's (1982) term, that rendered Bhutto desirable, I refuse the cultural conditions that make bodies matter only as sheer positivity or significations of individual empowerment. I queer the intelligibility that produced Bhutto as the proper subject of democracy by explicitly, transgressively, perversely and politically drawing attention to her body. The pernicious production of Bhutto as symbolic of democracy relied on her body, even as these structures of gazing (straight) at her disavowed such corporeal interests (or only affiliated with it insofar as it fetishized difference), making it exist and not exist at the same time.

How could the Western media have managed Bhutto's (liberal) feminist body and subjectivity without turning her into a mystical beauty queen of the orient: a restrained, coiffed, accessorized, elite, beautiful woman attached to a bloody legacy of democratic attempts in Pakistan, only to die in that same effort? It couldn't have. Mediated by metaphors and semantic grids, Bhutto was visually organized to animate perceptions of freedom for Pakistani women, but this was little more than a fantasy instituted and inscribed by a particular set of corporeal gestures that named her as free and modern and through which the dominant gaze imagined both democracy and women's rights in Pakistan. Whether unconsciously reproduced or deliberately crafted to appeal to the psychic contradictions and ambivalent desires of her spectators, the paradox of Bhutto's framing comes from the recesses of our most sedimented, unquestioned notions about gender and power, or (proper) democracy and (acceptable) *otherness*.

The general consensus in political discourse that concedes sexuality to the *other*, the queer, crumbles here as political life, feminine aesthetic,

Four. Is There a Queer Democracy? Or—Stop Looking Straight

and imperial scripts submerge around the popularly accepted framings of Bhutto. Constructing its substance through varying points on the female body that can be marked as democratic, through gendered behavior that sharpens the modernity of Pakistani nation-state or renders it dangerous, and through feminine sexuality that serves the nation and hetero-patriarchy simultaneously or enables their fragility; hetero-democracy plays on the intricate filaments between patriarchy, imperialism, sexuality and gender. By queering the discursive construction of Bhutto, I've pointed to the libidinal mechanisms and practices through which democracy and feminine freedom are imagined. I have sought to render lucid the link between heterosexual gazing and empire building as well as the centrality of Bhutto's public visualities to a bodily life that cannot be theorized away.

Five

"Chicks with Sticks"
Pleasure, Subversion and Insubordination in Female Political Subjectivity in Pakistan

In July 2007, a year marked as one of the most violent in Pakistan,[1] the infamous events of the Lal Masjid (Red Mosque) in Islamabad unfolded and the country took center stage in the global political theatre. The Lal Masjid became the site of a violent weeklong siege between the mosque's seminary students and the Pakistani military when the students of Jamia Hafza Madrasa, the enjoining religious school for women, rose in a violent resistance against what they perceived as foreign impositions of secularism and immorality. The Lal Masjid's two affiliated seminaries embarked on vigilante raids throughout the capital to stop what they called "un-Islamic activities," such as DVD vendors, barber shops and a Chinese-run massage parlor. This uprising began when female students abducted three Pakistani women accused of running a brothel and six Chinese masseuses who were employed there, claiming initially that they were only attacking Chinese girls who were prostitutes and CD shops who sold pornography.[2] They released them the next day,[3] but this action paved the way for the final confrontation, the siege of the Mosque and Madrasa by the Pakistani military, which the Islamic activists met with violent resistance.

While the standoff between the Lal Masjid and then-Musharraf's administration involved thousands of Islamic activists, at the frontlines

Five. "Chicks with Sticks"

were more than a hundred veiled women. The *BBC* (Hasan 2007) tells us that "The security personnel were met by baton-wielding women, who refused to let them enter the mosque or seminary compound." In the *New York Times*, Somini Sengupta (2007) reported that "shortly before the siege began, female students had come out of the school, draped in black burqas, waving bamboo sticks and taunting troops stationed nearby. The Pakistani news media dubbed them "chicks with sticks." The veiled female students demanded the resignation of the then current Pakistani administration and advocated an Islamic regime that would reinstate Islamic morality and return Pakistan to a state of Islamic purism. Despite the visibility and activity of the female students, when the events came to an end with the death of over 70 male students and the recovery of six women's bodies (veiled and burnt), the press released a statement that these women were held against their will and their bodies burned. These women were described by both their Islamic counterparts and their oppositional journalist parties as martyrs and/or militants. The final note as the events faded into Pakistan's now infamous militant Islamic history was uncertainty as to whether these women, those dead and those who surrendered, were "freedom fighters" or "victims."

As a globally publicized event, the Lal Masjid incidents brought to front and center a fantastic fear of today's times: veiled Muslim women who engage in abrasive, anti–American, pro–Pakistan political action to their death. Every image put forth of the Lal Masjid event was inflected with provocative media queries. Are these women victims or are they political actors? Are they pawns of a tight, un-nuanced patriarchy or are they the new agents of anti–American violence? Should we fear them or fold them into our democratic embrace? Can they be disciplined, empowered, made into recognizable modern subjects?

In this chapter, I analyze the Lal Masjid photographic discourses to elucidate how media narrations and visualities function as mechanisms of power that discipline subjects in Pakistan, resolidifying notions of dangerous nations and paranoid citizenship. I argue that the U.S., as a heteronormative nation, relies on, benefits from and eroticizes (repressed) fe/male terrorists. Throughout this book, I have identified representation as a key mechanism of power and pleasure, albeit one that is neither always consistent nor neat. Like Mai and Bhutto, I conceptualize the Lal Masjid women as *erotic nationals*—feminized, racialized subjects whose political practices are seen as exceptional and transgressive, on sexual and gender lines, and in ways that are fetishized and disavowed by the

U.S. state. These female martyrs are, in a number of way, a terrific coda in that they offer, in a sense, an antidote to the powerful (but often depressing) objectification and fetishization of Pakistani women. However, even here, the dominant representation of these martyrs by the media, as I will discuss, enacts a significant failure. These female martyrs carry profound implications for the ways in which liberatory and decolonial politics and practice are imagined because they destabilize liberal-humanist constructions of freedom through secularity and agency through autonomy. But such critical nuance went remiss, and instead, these women were disciplined through both brute force and paranoid visual rhetoric. The Lal Masjid women martyrs, I argue, demand a nuanced analysis that neither dismisses them as naively indoctrinated actors nor hails them as anti-colonial heroines.

My goal in this chapter is twofold. In the first part of my analysis, I work to reveal the erotic underbelly of seeing and narrating these martyrs, keeping taut the tension between the visual and the paranoid. I move from a deconstruction of this dominant gaze to a queer reading to show that the veiled martyrs of the proffer a continuity between the revolutionary women (we have always seen but dismissed in colonial battles from British India to French Algeria) and the contemporary feminine, racialized *other* who transforms herself from oppressed *other* to transgressive political subject.

Muslim Women as Fighters or Victims: Beyond the Binary

As I've argued, post–9/11 visual culture points to submerged histories of racist and colonialists violence that continue to resonate in the ways the Muslim *other* is imagined, desired and, and in the case of Lal Masjid women, destroyed (Jarmakani 2008; Williams, 2010). Significantly, this violence is justified through a narrative discourse of paranoia, a paranoia that revolves around particular bodies and subjects, aesthetics and freedoms (Foucault 1977; Williams 2010). In the case of the Lal Masjid, the colonial and neocolonial trope of the veiled Muslim woman was central to the production of the events. To the extent that the veil is an index of social oppression and political exclusion, Muslim women who practice covering in various ways become spectacle for Western

Five. "Chicks with Sticks"

states, as both a grotesque parody of antiquated gendered oppression but also eroticized symbols of the possibilities of Western freedom, where the unveiling of their bodies becomes a vested act of political interest.

Shahnaz Khan (2001: genders.org/33) argues that the "archetypal image of the veiled woman, even when accompanied by a speaking subject remains limited to the immediate sensory experience of what it is like to be confined." Joan Scott (2007) argues in *The Politics of the Veil*, that the "culture wars" in France over the veil provided fodder for neoliberal rationalities, servicing the dissolution of borders (where the veil functioned as Muslim border protection) as well as the expansion of forms of surveillance and identification (where the veil kept women from being *seen* and *sexualized* subjects by and for the state). That the French state is so vested in the clothing of Muslim women shows that the body is a symbolic fiction with performative power and symbolic/discursive efficiency feared by the state and, hence, subject to political forms of order (Butler 1993; Grosz 2000). Frantz Fanon's (1965) work directly implicates French colonial attitudes and strategies concerning the veil in Algeria. He argues that the colonialists' goal was "converting the woman, winning her over to foreign values, wrenching her free from her status," as a means of "shaking up the native man" and gaining control of him. There is long historical recognition that colonialists from French Algeria to the Indian subcontinent used women (and their bodies, sexualities, etc.) to demoralize/colonize the men.

Recall, here, Nicholas Kristoff's clear interest in Mai's clothing as demarcating her potential freedom or backwardness.

The potential of Muslim women to undo the state merely by their physical veiled presence speaks to a ferocious paranoia embedded in neoliberal state formations. The hysteria around the veil and its supposed associated with oppression has risen to political commonsense in the West, from France, to Germany, to the U.S, crafting a strategically and globally visible space for Muslim women. The continued furor of Muslim veiling practices in the secular West demonstrates that veiled women complicate the relationship between visibility and freedom.[4] Indeed, neoliberal globalization has transformed the politics of visibility and naming, where the symbolics of being a *seen* subject, have cleared the ground for discursive systems (from empire to the nation-state) that seek heightened opportunity for surveillance.

Of course, such neoliberal formulations of freedom jettison actual political realities and elide the dynamic political subjectivities that complicate the gendered and sexualized terrain of empire and political violence (Mernissi 2005; Mahmoud 2006). Treating political martyrs, or even suicide bombers as delusional, brainwashed figures dismisses the political realities that create the conditions of such forms of violence. Ghassen Hage (2003) demonstrates that Western approaches to suicide bombings versus the violence of colonial domination reveals a form of symbolic violence that shapes our understanding of what constitutes as ethical and legitimate violence. Hage's point highlight that what can be said about Muslim violence against the U.S. (as well as Muslim on Muslim violence) maintains the internal cohesiveness of the Master narrative regarding Muslim women, despite historical evidence that runs counter.

Because state power has historically always been imagined through hegemonic masculinity (Sjoberg and Gentry 2007) veiled Muslim women as political actors have either been completely ignored or are used to prop up narratives that define their actions as irrational. As a state-identified being, however, the body of the male citizen is fully unfolded and made complete. While, the Sovereign may bear a masculinized face, inversely the nation itself is feminized as mother/woman—recall the *National Geographic* that uses a woman's lowered/covered face as symbol of Pakistan's struggle for a "soul." Frantz Fanon's (1963) analysis of Algerian women's role in the revolution against France, conversely, lays bare the radical role Muslim Algerian women played in nationalist battles. Fanon moves Muslim female subjects from their perceived domestic and sexual passivity to public and revolutionary activity. Naming her as "woman-arsenal," Fanon (1963, 58) tells us the veil functioned as anti-colonial camouflage to carry various essentials (such as arms, food, communications, etc....) for the revolution.

In their analysis of Palestinian women's role in war, Laura Sjoberg and Caron Gentry (2007) argue that Palestinian groups often characterize women's participation in martyrdom attacks as a sign that women are equal in their society. The counter-narrative in Western responses is that gender emancipation through political violence is simply a continuation of their traditional, subordinated role in society. A number of feminist scholars argue that female martyrs do not unsettle gender lines because their actions take place within the framework of masculinist organizations. Likewise, during the Lal Masjid battle, Muslim women's involvement served to underscore the desperation of Pakistani society and the impossibility of diplomatic settlements with Pakistan. Involving

Five. "Chicks with Sticks"

women made Pakistan more uncivilized, legitimizing the continued and insidious use of force in the region. But it also fundamentally marked, and continues to mark, the region as a threat to America (Bhattherchaya 2008). But to say that gender or nation is not at all recoded through these actions is mistaken. This cultural conflict over whether martyrdom liberates or oppresses women trumps any real discourse regarding these subjects and elides alternative imaginaries of freedom or subjectivity.

Because liberal humanism defines the figure of the veiled woman as the quintessential oppressed figure, the radical disruption offered by these women is foreclosed on, rendering them unthinkable as political subjects. Within the nostalgic imperial imaginary, the image of the Lal women as acting (rather than docile) and politicized (rather than privatized) sustains a logic that produces brown women as simultaneously savable and politically impossible. Hence, a parallel narrative to Muslim women as faux political subjects is the increasingly intertwined description of their political actions and indeed, themselves, as sexualized (see, e.g., Sjoberg and Gentry 2007). Jacqueline Zita (1998) argues that the gendering of stories of violent women is a representation of male dread of women or more specifically, male anxiety over female control. I will suggest that the media's labeling the Lal Masjid martyrs "chicks with sticks" as well as the political actions that the women themselves performed with regard to the sexual regulation of other females simultaneously evokes and effaces imperial erotics, raising questions over the politics of agency and political subjectivity.

This backdrop of gender, race and border politics as central but sublimated dimensions of the war on terror constitute Pakistan and the Lal Masjid events as a particularly brutal case to explore the representations and possibilities of Pakistani female political subjectivity. Throughout this book, I have shown how the very fabric of the war on terror has simultaneously revealed the deep narcissism of the west and contradictorily opened up possibilities for the emergence of distinct unruly, fragmented subjectivities (Puar 2007; Mahmoud 2005). Veena Das and Deborah Poole (2004) characterize unruly subjects as those who are insufficiently socialized into laws of gender or nation, and hence, possibly undo the state even as they simultaneously utilize the state. Frantz Fanon (1963) points out that subaltern resistance and revolution is shaped by the simultaneous and contradictory coexistence of both anti-colonial conservatism and anti-colonial radicalism. Saba Mahmoud (2005), in her ethnographic study of pious Egyptian women who actively construct and participate in an Islamic movement, demonstrates how politicized Muslim women's agency cannot be seen as fixed in advance but rather as emerging through specific modes of being, responsibility and effectiveness (Mahmoud 2005). Mahmoud challenges the modernist project that seeks to categorize these pious and veiled Muslim women as nonpolitical subjects or antifeminist and instead repositions these women from docile bodies to active, agentic subjects. Agency, Mahmoud (2005) tells us, should be understood as framed within discourses of domination and subordination that create the conditions for women's political enactment. Such a characterization of resistance is external to Western romanticizations which frame resistance as a product of individual agency.[5] The relationship, then, between subscription to political Islam and/or the suppression of women's civil rights is neither absolute nor linear. With such considerations in mind, let us turn to three dominant images of the Lal Masjid events to interrogate the ways power, as Landau and Kaspin (2002:12) write, "is hidden in ways of seeing."

Visual Subjects/Violent Gazes: The Lal Masjid Women in Photographs

> *We must all be of one and the same mind when we look upon the photographic evidence. It is in these photographs that Americans can meet on the common ground of their beloved traditions. Here we are all united at the shrine.*
> —Francis Trevelyan Miller, *1911*

As the Lal Masjid event came to a close, every press pondered on the role of these women. *BBC's* (Bano 2009) query capture's this concern, "But why are more and more families sending their girls to religious schools? Are they linked to Islamic fundamentalism or was the Lal Masjid a one off?" This question, of course, fits with broader media strategies that tend to render unexplained phenomena less dangerous through the narrative of romanticized exceptionalism. It also, however, fits the odd political subjectivity that the Lal Masjid brought forward. The strikingly insistent presence of both the female body and the woman subject in the event and the political discourse that followed, begs the following questions. What is *seen* in these photographs and what effect, visually and

Five. "Chicks with Sticks"

epistemologically, did they have on the imperial gaze? What kinds of subjectivities are incited and denied?

Three of the most dominantly circulated images come from both the Associated Press and *Pakistan Today*—images that were also reproduced by the BBC and the *New York Times* (http://www.pakistantoday. com.pk/2014/12/30/national/father-of-brainwashed-jamia-hafsa-student-moves-sc/; http://www.apimages.com/metadata/index/Pakistan-Radical-Mosque/3e4e9aeb9ef34a24856f5bd730e0b1a0/334/0; http://www.apimages.com/metadata/index/Pakistan/213da52a248440c48cd9f87d53e66ff9/300/0). In the first two images of the Lal Masjid, we see masses of women, shrouded in full black *niqab*, carrying bamboo sticks—raised sometimes in the air as they pound the dirt floor with them. The women's faces are not visible. The viewer only sees their eyes, which the Western media tend to describe as dark, angry or emotionless (Sengupta 2007). The image is either taken from a distance, encompassing the masses of female bodies "draped in black burqa," or through honing closely in on one face to see, as Somini Sengupta (2007) of the *New York Times* describes, "lively eyes sparkling out of a black burqa." The camera is positioned so that the masses feel endless and overwhelming. In the first image, we see rows of women standing around one another forming a protest, their bodies uniformly covered, their arms raised holding erect bamboo sticks, the dirt floor under their feet, the gates a mosque (denoted by the Arabic lettering over their heads) behind them, a megaphone pressed against one woman's mouth. In the second photograph, the camera is angled above, looking down at the masses of veiled women, as they peel forward in protest.

These photographs invariably mobilize the colonial trope of looking at the veiled female, where the power of the gaze is aligned with (unveiled) whiteness. For example, one is a close-up photograph of a *niqab*-clad woman, her eyes staring into the camera. The image lends itself to an eerie quality of the *othered* woman subject, one that is simultaneously curious and suspect. This photograph, specifically, figures into media-driven iconography rooted in fetishism, a fetish repeatedly displayed through the landscape of Muslim women's bodies. Every element of the photograph strategically elicits a fetishistic response from the viewer, naturalizing the hetero-erotic and the imperial gaze. By honing in on the eyes, the dominant gaze lays claim to the undeniable pleasures afforded to those who can *look* at iconic, Muslim femininity. Indeed the journalists' description, "lively eyes sparkling out of the black burqa," juxtaposed to the black burqa reveals the tortured relation between the imperial gaze, which eroticizes the *other* and imperial initiatives, i.e., the war on terror, which demonizes the *other*. This brief but evocative description by the *New York Times* foregrounds my central argument that these martyrs, despite their political action, were folded into a narrative that is at once hetero-erotic and racist. The Muslim woman in this photograph, once again, emerges as the quintessential veiled woman and the exotic whore (Naber 2006).

In other images, the playful focus on the dark eyes is replaced by a fear-encoded shot of the veiled women. In one, we see three women, wearing the burqa—two making the peace sign with their hands and the third holding a bamboo stick. We see only their hands and eyes, which are sober, serious, stern. This image was taken after the events came to an end, when the Lal Masjid women were demanding the re-opening of the mosque. In another, we see the veiled female masses, conglomerating, protesting. Recall the *Newsweek* image that displayed masses of angry Muslim men and the precise ideological and material effects of such photographic representation. Similarly, the highly specific and deeply strategic visual signs in these photograph, such as the suspended bamboo sticks, the Arabic lettering in the background, the unpaved, dirt floors, *niqabs* blending into one another, the facelessness of the women, the megaphones, then endless masses, operate within a discursive field of power deployed to achieve certain ends—feminine irrationality, Muslim barbarism, the dangerous Muslim nation. They reiterate. They simplify. They agitate. They create an illusion of consensus. By looking we experience all we need to know.

Described by American, British, Indian and Pakistan media with phrases such *"burqa brigade," "baton-wielding," "fearsome, stick-wielding, burke-clad young women....pouring out of the mosque,"* these photographs and accompanying text secures the discursive tension of the dangerous Muslim nation even as it complicates dominates readings that vilify Muslim men as only dangerous and Muslim women as only oppressed. Viewing the images from first to last renders visible the orientalists' ambivalence in gazing at the other, seesawing from (erotic) pleasure to (political) fear (Said 1979). This split between pleasure and fear encodes Muslim female bodies as desirable only if readable as oppressed, mobilizing a political fantasy first articulated by Laura Bush in 2001 when she stated Muslim women needed saving. Bush's nostalgically evoked notion of "the oppressed Muslim woman" gives rise to the acuity of the camera's gaze, constructing each image as signifiers of Islamic oppression, backwardness, irrationality. In other words, the viewer is confident that "free" actors are not being represented. The visual technologies of the veil, then, produce the subjective impossibilities of freedom. The Lal Masjid women, as unintelligible subjects (or intelligible only as oppressed), become the perfect foil through which to imagine the Western liberal rational, unveiled, woman.

The Erotics of the Lal Masjid Discourse

The Lal Masjid women complicate the story of women's oppression within Muslim societies, inducing an exceptional (though invariably ephemeral) opportunity to break with the status quo. But what's most obvious here is that, despite their political activity, they are not dealt with as political subjects. In a classic juxtaposition to Benazir Bhutto, Ginny Dougary (2010) of the *Huffington Post*, refers to the Lal masjid women as schoolgirls: "Meanwhile in the same capital, ostensibly the very stronghold of government power, we witness the strange spectacle of stick-waving, burkha-clad schoolgirls—like a fundamentalist version of St Trinian's—kidnapping suspected brothel-keeping madams ... and then the police officers themselves who came to release the captives." Even the state machines that had to contend with these women through violent means, referred to the martyrs through the conventional language of femininity. The *Prospect UK*, (Hoodbhoy 2007) tells us, "Even as the writ of the state was being openly defied, the chief negotiator appointed by Musharraf described the "burqa brigade" militants as "our daughters" against whom "no operation could be contemplated." The state's unwillingness to recognize these women's political subjectivity and the fetishistic reduction to ideological caricatures such "daughter" and "burqa-brigade," downplays the possibility of them as *really* threatening.

But an even more convoluted visual and discursive formation can be excavated here. The appropriation of these women as daughters by the state is troubled by the recurring motif produced by the media: "chicks with sticks." Both *BBC* and a number of Pakistani media outlets such as *Daily Times, All Things Pakistan* and *Daily Star* labeled the women protestors in this way. According to the *New Yorker* (Dalwymple 2007), these English-language jokes were quickly abandoned when the women kidnapped prostitutes, threatened video-store owners, and made bonfires of books, videocassettes, and DVDs that they regarded as un-Islamic. The media as we know carry their own agenda—to sell newspapers and find readers—thus making sensationalized language part of the competitive game to increase readership (Tagg 1988). But the media's persistence in naming these women "chicks with sticks," and then later denying responsibility for this phrase, must be more deeply interrogated, not just for effect, but for intent.

As I've discussed, in these photographs, every visual trope enacted to capture the events of the Lal Masjid relied upon (Muslim) femininity as dominantly understood—erotic, repressed, protected, and shrouded. But, to say that the Lal Masjid events were marked by a sexual discourse is to, at once, say too much and not enough. Following Foucault (1978), technologies of sex create and regulate, rather than reflect, the sexual bodies that they name. As both a technology of representation and a technology of power, the phrase "chicks with sticks" demonstrates an interplay of eroticism and political dismembership, simultaneously dis-identifying these women as terrorists and reifying them (through jest) as women.

The discursive formations that render these women visible do so, not to destabilize the dimension of political life that seeks to make the body irrelevant, but with a *joussance* associated with constituting female bodies as operational national texts, where both international media and state machines gender the conflict and its participants, obscure the political reality, and aestheticize political action as a ménage a trios of the nation, woman and God. As such, these subjects come to represent *erotic nationals*, subjects produced through the hetero-patriarchal gaze, which frames their political action as an eroticized, sensationalized, fantasized spectacle. The erotic subjectivity afforded these women is the simultaneous effect of neocolonial politics and hetero-patriarchal national discourses, over-determining the use/utility of these feminine subjects/bodies as futile but *fuckable*. As daughters, these women can be folded into a normative structure of gender and sexuality, but as "chicks with sticks," they emerge as erotic subjects pronounced by fetishized markers of embodied femininity. The phrase "chicks with sticks" cleverly interprets these women as libidinal, where sexual purity is replaced with sexual deviance, the mundane with fetish, and the Pakistani state with an hetero-erotic empire.

Landau and Kaplan (2002:26) argue, "every unit of meaning, and not just every image, is a public crossroads of histories of interpretations."

Five. "Chicks with Sticks"

The visual and decontextualized photographic narrative of the Lal Masjid reveals this with immediate clarity. In the semantic shift from "veiled women of the Lal Masjid protested" to "chicks with sticks," the veil as a symbol of sexual modesty is deemphasized, if not completely bastardized. The phrase simultaneously genders and eroticizes the representations of these women, while also rendering them vulnerable, hence less threatening. As chicks, these women don't possess a political subjectivity and are reduced to gendered metaphors that feminize them. The lingual fantasy of these women as chicks demonstrates that the female body is incapable of being viewed through a neutral lens. It is always and completely sexed by the dominant gaze (Bordo 1993; Grosz 1990).

Second, the use of this phrase reduces these women to the specularity of their sexual bodies. Here, the fantasy of these women as "chicks" illustrates the need to produce and secure a nondangerous subject positioning through the most familiar trope of all—reducing women to sex objects. The phrase functions to make them impotent as political actors; as "chicks," they cease to be dangerous, except in their licentious potential for seduction. The specific visual strategies of distancing the camera from its subjects, the subjects blending into one another, the masses of black burqas, the pounding sticks, the open mouths against the language of the media, "chicks with sticks" bespeaks the possibility of Muslim barbarism even as it caricaturizes it. Even here then, the barbarism of the Muslim society is both incited and mocked, as the media demonstrates through its jocular phrase that beneath the veiled, angry woman is a body to be *fucked*.

Third, the figurative imagery embedded in this phrase tactically serves the masculinist and imperial fantasy of disciplining the colonial subject and, in reverse, being (sexually) disciplined by that same subject (Pierce and Rao 2006). The women must lose political power in order to gain sexual prowess, becoming the subject Orientalist tropes have long relied upon—subjects of sexual arousal while being subjected to sexual discipline. The phrase "chicks with sticks" also seems a play on "chicks with dicks," linking them with lesbians and transgendered people, and more broadly, some abject notion of queerness and aggressive female sexuality. Here, the erotic is both enshrined in the language used to describe the women and inadvertently denied as the women are increasingly read as politically dangerous. Or as Mulvey (1989) argues, looking at the monster constitutes the monster.

The language employed by the media makes it apparent that the female body in political space is confined to patriarchal and heteronormative narratives, even when it attempts to transcend these borders. As "chicks with sticks," images of the Lal Masjid women become sites of social and psychic satisfaction for the dominant viewer, affording the global gaze the voyeuristic illusion of penetrating the "enigma of Muslim women," but in ways that do not compromise visual control over these subjects. The construction of these women as "chicks with sticks," while undoubtedly rooted in colonial longings directed at the colonized *other*, ironically resonates with a familiar subject performance in Western politics—political women in the U.S. have long been reduced to their sexual bodies.

Moreover, it is important to note, despite the fact that their womanhood (in contrast to that of the prostitutes) operates within the realm of state-sanctioned heterosexuality, this does little to secure the grounds for their political insubordination. Instead, their political insubordination (to the imperial state of affairs) is imagined as beyond the boundaries of heterosexuality, slipping into deviant, alternative sexualities that both dominant nationalisms and the U.S. heteronormative state seek to control. As Khalid Khan (2007), writing for Pakistani newspaper *Dawn*, states, in the Lal Masjid, we "see madressah girls stealing the limelight from their male counterparts in Pakistan. They do not speak softly, and they carry big sticks.... This time around womenfolk are the harbinger of Islamic sharia or a metropolitan jihad without charismatic leaders." Similarly, Tahira Abdulla (2009) of *Himal*, a South Asian magazine, states that "the scenes of hordes of stick-wielding, shouting, black-garbed young women on the seminary's ramparts, provoking the law-enforcement machinery, will long be etched in the region's collective memory." Such sentiments reveal a form of gendered agency that disrupts the representation of the normative Pakistani female subject. But in describing the Lal Masjid insurgency through feminine reductions, such as speaking softly, lacking charismatic leadership—a trait long associated with (white) masculinity, and "chicks with sticks," these statements repeatedly enact a refusal to see the nuanced complexity of Pakistani women's violent political action.

Significantly, the media and state's attempt to cast these female political actors as erotic abruptly forecloses on the queer possibilities opened up by the space of politicized female homosociality and corporeality. Subjugating these women to the erotic functions as a crucial mode of discipline and production of these subjects as intelligible only as a form

Five. "Chicks with Sticks"

of ribaldry. The gender transgression of these women, as political actors, is successfully reinscripted as oppression rather than political intent, erotic rather than transformative. The queer potential of the Lal Masjid women is replaced by the primacy of the female body, keeping in tact all the ways nation, politics and gender are all "weighed down" in de Beauvoir's (1952: xxiii) words, by the female body.

Transgressive Subjects: Rereading the Lal Masjid Women

> When it comes to the concomitant question of the consciousness of the subaltern, the notion of what the work cannot say becomes important. In the semiosis of the social text, elaborations of the insurgency stand in place of "utterance.
> —Gayatri Spivak, 1988, 91

> They came into the private women's quarters of Mosque, with grenades and tears gas, twenty-odd commandos. We had been threatened, our children had been threatened, our mosque had been invaded by the military ... were we supposed to greet them with flowers?
> —Shahid [Jamia Hafza woman responds when asked why the women needed to resort to arming themselves with sticks], 2007, *GeoTV* interview

In an interview with *GeoTV* (2007), the Mawlana of the Lal Masjid, Abdul Rashid Ghazi, said, "these women were faced with military weapons and highly-trained commandos, but they are nothing less than commandos themselves." In Ghazi's words, we hear a possible articulation of an anticolonial project that centers on a complex model of female Islamic subjectivity (Interview with *GeoTV*, geotv.org, *Mere Mutabik*, translated—*In My Opinion*). Likewise, the woman's above statement and Spivak's (1988) point compels us to engage these women's insurgencies as a point of subaltern agency that defy liberal conventions of resistance. How do the Lal Masjid women queer empire's contest over proper political subjectivity and the (im)possibilities of freedom?

In the events of the Lal Masjid, the women on the frontlines utilized the liminal status of the veiled women, an embodiment of oppression and tradition rendered abject by liberal-humanist codes, in order to comment on the colonized status of Pakistan and Islam. These women rework the ambivalent figure of the veiled women into a feminist predecessor of contemporary anti-colonial subjectivity. Their use of the hyperbolic femininity that is presumed with the donning of the *niqab* unharnesses the pleasures of dominant representations from its disciplinary and regulatory role. Indeed, these women enact a queer appropriation of Muslim women in public space—where they are agents of, rather than subject to, violence.

Returning to the Associated Press images, both photographs attempt to capture an endless number of veiled women. The endlessness of women in full niqabs suggests a menace of sorts, an intimidating population. Arguably, these two images of the women martyrs are a realistic representation of women's corporeal force in political space. Politicized religious nationalism can be interpreted as an insistent, powerful force with a life of its own—female corporeality writ large. These photographs reflects the psychological reality of neocolonialism, rage turned protest,—a state these women are unwilling to distinguish from death itself (Fanon 1963). In the words of Fanon (1963:16), these women may be dominated, but they are not domesticated. They deliver a message whose poignancy is conveyed by the female body.

To be sure, I am not speaking of corporeality in the abstract. Rather I am directly concerned with the ways in which these bodies are materialized and the political consequences of that materialization. One of the key organizing principles of Deleuze and Gauttari's (1984) work is to ask the question, "What can a body do?" This question invites us to restage questions of agency and to think at a different ontological level about how the body can act/move or not. This is a notoriously difficult ground—this taking up of the politico-analytical force of the female martyrs' bodies, and perhaps largely, the bodies of women who don't seamlessly mold into the neoliberal/neocolonial fantasy of empowerment. The Lal Masjid women proffer a self who makes the materiality of her body highly relevant to the political schema and to her political knowledge. In so doing, these women rupture the codification of Cartesian empowered subjectivity—an empowerment that rests on the excision of the corpus from the ideal subject. Indeed, it is not a stretch to argue that these female martyrs—veiled women occupying the public space to make a political statement—are saying that we are not separate from our bodies; we *are* our bodies.

Five. "Chicks with Sticks"

BBC (2007), for example, quoted a young Lal Masjid student, saying, "The 18-year-old told the *BBC Urdu Service* that she was not held hostage by militants but had willingly remained behind during the weeklong siege. The woman, who asked not to be named, said she was prepared to carry out a suicide attack to defend the mosque." Like the Jamia Hafsa women quoted in the opening, this woman shifts the image of the pure, unsullied and oppressed Muslim woman to an emblem of female resistance. The mere fact that these women met the military armed with sticks (and prepared to die) in an effort to protect both the physical parameters of the Mosque and the religio-political borders of their work and families denaturalizes the image of the Muslim male as the quintessential anti-Western rebel and replaces terrorists iconography with ambivalent and gender queer figures. The opening statement by the Jamia Hafsa woman, "were we supposed to greet them with flowers?" empties feminine symbolism even as it uses it, as these women chose to meet violence with violence. In this event of intense decolonial dramatization, like Fanon's (1963:50) Algerian woman, the Lal Masjid women "rise directly to the level of tragedy."

Alongside the politicization of the Muslim feminine corporeality, these martyrs challenge hegemonic, neoliberal constructions of subjectivity. If subjectivity is defined epistemologically as knowable through observation and confession; ethically, as moderate, autonomous, civilized; and technically, as the regimens and practices we do to improve and become autonomous, free and fulfilled—then these martyrs confront all dimensions of Western subjectivity. The female martyrs in the Lal Masjid events were nameless, often spoken about or referred to as a group, a mass or a collective. The language and the gaze of the press lump these women together as "fearsome, stick-wielding, burka-clad young women ... pouring out of the mosque" (Dalwymple 2007). But even here, the policing gaze cannot fully control the body it seeks to.

In this regard, the Lal Masjid martyrs maintain a complicated in/visibility—they are *seen* as a (dangerous) collective but remain *unseen* as named individuals. In their refusal to be named, insofar as they operated as a collective and asked to not be named, and in the media's refusal to present them as named individuals, these martyrs incite Cold War paranoia now translated to fit within the global security regime and neoliberal world order of today. Their quasi-public in/visibility demonstrates the empire's inability to govern their private selves, their intimate subjectivities, their interior lives (Rose 1989). Their techniques of self—collectivity over individuality, inter-relationalism over autonomy, radicalism over moderation—endanger Western individualism and therefore, Western formulas around freedom. Their collective visibility, over named individual subjectivity, renders them unrecognizable. But, in becoming unrecognizable political monsters, these women deterritorialize the nation and the white racial state, a deterretorialization which involves more than simply undermining or doing away with hierarchy. To deterritorialize is to dismantle the subject, disorganize the body and even to destabilize the state.

The feminist organization, Shirkat Gah, released a report on the Lal Masjid events that spoke to complex reasons Pakistani women were drawn to the Jamia Hafsa. Kamila Hyat (2007) writes:

> The Jamia Hafsa appears to have served primarily to meet a key economic need in society. Families of young women, and in some cases young women themselves, including domestic workers, appear to have turned to it because it offered what was not always available to them in the world outside: Food, shelter, clothing, respectability and learning. The realities the Jamia Hafsa exposed about society were restricted not only to the matter of 'liberals' versus 'extremists'. Rather, a bright spotlight was directed towards the factors that have led to madrassahs mushrooming in Pakistan. These institutions serve to reduce the socio-economic burden on families. The poor condition of public sector schools, which have declined markedly over the last two decades, means that a 'madrassah' is a truly tempting option for many. This of course is all the more true in the case of girls, with the Jamia Hafsa—and other madrassahs like it—offering a convenient, socially acceptable place at which to depose of them, and thus lessen the strain on family finances.

Despite the nuances introduced by the Shirkat Gah report, well-known Pakistani feminist writer and blogger, Afiya Zia, explains the activities of the Jamia Hafza were largely mocked, dismissed or reduced to patriarchal victimization by civil society members, most of whom are the liberal elite. Zia (2008) writes:

> Most civil society members were disturbed by the threat to liberal lifestyles, rather than looking at this occupation as a politics of protest that challenged the state. The Jamia Hafsa women, who wore complete black veils and carried bamboo sticks in their occupation of the mosque library, were mocked by the liberal, English-language media as the "veiled brigade" or "chicks with sticks".... This tendency tends to elide over and ignore the serious political spaces they have come to occupy. Progressive women's groups, as expected, made more salient statements on this incident, bringing out a historical perspective and linking extremist violence to the past thirty years of state policies.

Five. "Chicks with Sticks"

We can see a clear distinction in feminist thinkers who are trying to situate the Lal Masjid women actors within a discourse of resistance to both neoliberal and neocolonial practices in Pakistan. Zia's (2007) point and the Shirkat Gah report introduce a more compelling critique of both trans/national economic processes, which further disenfranchise women, and the nuanced political practices these women offer to transnational formations of gendered politics. But this critique extends into resistant cultural spaces as well. For example, let me note here that Pakistani artist, Naiza Khan, created a few provocative pieces around the female body and female armory, noting that "At Lal Masjid, for the first time one saw a seemingly strong women's force" (Perlez 2007). Khan has charted an exemplary independent path among the shifting currents of contemporary Pakistani art, producing an extended body of work exploring the sensuality and recalcitrance of the female body. "The Wardrobe," a provocative piece, is a series developed by the artist in response to the 2007 Islamabad Lal Masjid siege. In this series, Khan directly takes on the fatal and embodied resistance of the Lal Masjid women. Khan created a series of fabricated metal corsets and armor bodices that were both defensive and defiant, installations that grappled with the ways in which veiled female participation in violent political action dismantled the disembodied white, U.S. (and Pakistani) gaze and the authority of that gaze to determine another's ontological position in a racist and sexist typology. From organization work to individual activists and artists, we see the ways in which grassroots feminist work in Pakistan sheds light on the complex possibilities that went remiss in the state and media's inability to see these women (and their actions) as anything but deviant or downtrodden.

Clearly, the martyrs' role in the Lal Masjid battles intervened in dominant nationalists discourses of gender, subjectivity and empire. When the Lal Masjid women kidnapped Chinese prostitutes as a gesture of resistance to "foreign imposition of immorality," they catalogue a tacit critique of the racist amnesia that created Asian patterns of migration to Pakistan. Im/migration practices and politics in South Asia have direct roots in the global economic labor trade, which often divest immigrants of citizenship status, allocate them to short-term labor contract, often sexual in nature, and render them perpetual outsiders in Pakistan (Appadurai 1996). The displaced, deterritorialized and transient populations that constitute Pakistan after 9/11 drives the complex hierarchical organizations of the modern Pakistani nation-state even as its sexualized and racialized realities render the nation's borders fragile and unpredictable. Indeed, the erasure of the Chinese sex workers' voice from the Lal Masjid media discourses and the fact that the Chinese women were the most accessible markers of penetrative foreign policy to the Lal Masjid women is emblematic of these globalizing border practices that displace and demarcate citizenship on gender and sexual lines. The racialized feminization of labor under global capitalism bleeds into the martyrs' advocacy of a Pakistan that wants to disassociate with such effects of globalization, even as they utilize hetero-nationalisms to articulate their critique (Asad 2003; Appadurai 1996). As such, these women can be understood as protecting the borders of a nation from the threat of sexualized immigration, a reflection of neoliberal globalization that cannot be dismissed.

But recognizing the anti-globalization practices that possibly undergird the kidnapping does not attend to the question of the martyrs' responsibility for *othering* women even as they themselves may be victimized by global politics. Here, I turn to the question of the actual violence that the veiled women enact on the Chinese immigrants in Pakistan. The coercive kidnapping of the Chinese prostitutes was, by varying media accounts, described as lasting from twenty-four hours to three days and resulted in either the anti-climactic release of the Chinese women or a dramatic public confession after which they were released. Mostly, though, there is a general lack of knowledge of what took place in the Madrassa around the sex workers—we don't know how they were treated, we don't know how long they were held, we don't know anything. Media accounts are vague and, frankly, not focused on the kidnapping of the prostitutes.

This discursive invisibility of the Chinese prostitutes by the national and international media as well as the martyrs' kidnapping of these sex workers elucidates how the sexual/erotic operate as a particularly efficient and dangerous conduit for exercising power. But they are not parallel or analogous stories. They organized different forms of violence and exclusion and ordered different arenas of social and political action. The kidnapping of the Chinese prostitutes catalyzed military intervention into the Lal Masjid, even as this catalyzing event subsided into the margins of the public and global discourse. This narrative omission reveals both national and international discomfort with humanizing sex workers as well as the ideological refusal to provide them with liberal (celebrated) forms of visibility: Where now is the fanatic desire to render invisible subjects visible?

Five. "Chicks with Sticks"

Visibility, as I've shown throughout this book, is a complex system of permission and prohibition, of presence and absence. Hence, it is not a matter of accepting or rejecting the invisibility of the Chinese prostitutes. The political and affective modalities at play here, both in terms of the invisibility of the sex workers and the social violence inflicted on them by other women, are neither accidental nor wholly explainable. To contend with the fact the Lal Masjid women exercised, perhaps the most familiar form of patriarchal violence towards the Chinese prostitutes, is to recognize that the dogmatic positions of secularism and anti-secularism have always been concerned with women's bodies and sexuality, in ways that expand from violence to liberation. The martyrs violence towards the Chinese sex workers occurred on a terrain situated between patriarchy, secular-liberalism, capitalism, state terror, and the global war and the various and contradictory ambiguities, experiences, logics that accompany such events. On the other hand, the kidnapping of the Chinese prostitutes was deemed nonviolent or less important (by both the media and the state—it was reduced to a diplomatic issue), in part through the paradigmatic phrase, "chicks with sticks," which established the martyrs as less credible dangerous political subjects. In the end, both the Chinese sex workers and the Pakistani women martyrs were subject to familiar forms of patriarchal and imperial violence— their agency neutralized, dismissed, eroticized.

By tracing the gendered and sexualized exploitations and possibilities of the photographic representations of the Lal Masjid, I highlight the voyeuristic fantasy of politicized Muslim woman subjects and the ways in which both their violence against other women (i.e., the Chinese prostitutes) and their own eventual death (i.e., martyrdom or murder) is fetishized, eroticized and rendered unintelligible, indeed irrelevant. One of the most subversive aspects of the Lal Masjid women's is the way they resituate the materialist visual paradigm that refuses to *see* both their violence against other women (i.e., the Chinese prostitutes) and their own eventual death (i.e., martyrdom or murder). Perhaps, then, by refusing to ignore the panoply of politics these women enact and trouble, we can reinstate at least some of their radical work along gender, race, sex and visual lines.

Coda

Will the Real Pakistani Woman Please Stand Up?
Unhappy Archives and the Failure of Visual Culture

> *To be involved in political activism is thus to be involved in a struggle against happiness. Even if we are struggling for different things, even if we have different worlds we want to create, we might share what we come up against. Our activist archives are thus unhappy archives. Just think of the labor of critique that is behind us: feminist critiques of the figure of "the happy housewife;" Black critiques of the myth of "the happy slave"; queer critiques of the sentimentalisation of heterosexuality as "domestic bliss." The struggle over happiness provides the horizon in which political claims are made. We inherit this horizon.*
>
> —Sara Ahmed, The *Promise of Happiness*

The 1950s classic game show, *To Tell the Truth*, was popularly syndicated every decade until its final appearance in 2002. The show featured a panel of four celebrities attempting to correctly identify a described contestant (a person of some notoriety, ranging from *Roots* author, Alex Haley, to Frank Abagnale to Candie Lightner, founder of Mothers against Drunk Driving [MADD]). The primary contestant, the famous *somebody*,

Coda. Will the Real Pakistani Woman Please Stand Up?

was accompanied by two imposters, charlatans who pretended to be the central character. The object of the game was to try to fool the celebrities into voting for the two impostors. In the end, the real central character was revealed through a series of questions, with a climax of which was "will the real (x) please stand up?"

The show's central premise, and its emblematic phrase became part of popular culture, such as white rapper Eminem's 2005 hit single, "Will the Real Slim Shady Please Stand Up?" The phrase, now cemented in our cultural lexicon, evokes an irony circumvented by an overreliance on the real. This call of/for the "real" subject provides an opportunity to explore the meaning of authenticity, artificiality and the (in)stability of both. Indeed, the intent of the phrase, in both the colloquial field and in the theoretical context of this book, precludes and permits the authenticity and the materiality of the given subject. What draws me to this catch phrase is that it reveals that what we call "real" cannot be understood outside of the convergence of insinuation and simulation, containment and confession.

In titling my book, *Will the Real Pakistani Woman Please Stand Up?* I too play with this semantic gesture to underscore that what white neoliberal civilization often calls the real Pakistani woman, and more broadly the Muslim woman, is ultimately a white (wo)man's artifact—a real which simultaneously exists and doesn't exist, in each image, through each subject. In claiming to render Pakistan transparent through the canvas of the female body, the white racial state participates in what Alain Badiou (2003) identifies as "a passion for the Real," a real which culminates in theatre spectacle and fetish rather than in material reality, a real which is constituted by extreme violence rather than everyday social reality; thus, a real that can be characterized as the most vacuous of terms and the most precarious of identities. The very thought of the Pakistani woman being called to stand up and represent both a complex and fraught nation and the shifting, multifaceted narrative of woman increasingly through the medium of visual culture is an appropriation that at once energizes and reveals the structures of oppression through which she becomes both Pakistan and woman.

As sociologists, how do we rethink post–9/11 visual culture as a central story-telling device in a world where, as Avery Gordon (2008:49) tells us, "the real is no longer self-evident, where the social fact may be more properly understood as an artifact, where the depiction of cultural life is made problematic by the very mode of producing such a description?" How do we work through, acknowledge, understand the subtle varieties of freedom that these women's visual and visible stories suggest, e.g., the freedom of public protest, the freedom to present oneself as public figure? How do we attend to the structural and symbolic processes underlying bodily erasure and exposure, grievable bodies and ungrievable subjects, epitomized in the cultural fascination with the Taliban shooting victim Malala Yousafzai and other figures that emerge at the global neoliberal conjuncture of visual culture? Thus, I conclude with both a tentative and speculative discussion on the failures of visual culture and the (un)happy archives of the white racial state.

In/Visible Technologies: Sexing and Securitizing the Nation and the Body

I opened this book by saying the veracity of Pakistan only exists in the complex day-to-day realities and psychic affects that come with smell, taste, touch, and memories. In contrast throughout this book, I have shown how in the aftermath of 9/11, Pakistan's authenticity is announced through the technologies of visual production of/over brown fe/male bodies. This body becomes the most visible molecule through which the Pakistani nation-state is articulated, and hence surveyed, regulated, and disciplined. My attention to representational practices on Pakistan underscores how the frequent conflation of authenticity with specific kinds of national, gendered, and embodied performances informs and deforms the visual realm in which Pakistani subjects become real to us.

If Adrienne Rich (1979:199) has described the imposition of invisibility on women as "the attempt to fragment you, to prevent you from integrating love and work and feelings and ideas, with the empowerment that that can bring," then conversely, we learn from Spivak (1988) that the clearest available example of epistemic violence is the "remotely orchestrated, far-flung, heterogeneous project to constitute the colonial subject as other." I take both these feminist positions seriously, as they bring together my own inchoate suspicions and disappointments alongside my philosophical stammering. If Pakistani women's visibility must draw on imperial coordinates and war machineries to be intelligible, is it, then, wiser to secede to Deleuze (1968:87), when he said, "thus representation mediates everything but mobilizes and moves nothing?"

Coda. Will the Real Pakistani Woman Please Stand Up?

This history of assessing and reassessing the politics of visibility and visuality is of central importance when rethinking these photographic terrains as *not* a parochial matter confined to one field, but as part of a broader organization of knowledge and power on and over the brown body. While race and gender have to change in order to work as part of the regulative apparatuses of a powerful state, they remain connected to earlier histories of exploitation, exoticism, violence and governmentality. Thus, I have come to understand the project of empire as not simply of conquest and pillage, of moral and political paternalism, but also invested in a broad orientation of how to familiarize itself with the *other*. What is seen as paradoxically inimical to the Western "self" must be refashioned, often under the teleological process of improvement, a process I've illuminated in my three visual fields. While one figure is reduced to a stable site of shame and abjection, another is deployed in the name of American excellence and symbolic democracy, and yet others are offered up as the monsters/whores of this war. My analysis has shown that no gendered or racialized body reaches the (impossible) mean; all are subject to discursive violence, encouraged to go deeper into the rabbit-hole of racial projects and self-correction. Chris Weedon (1997) poignantly captures this notion when she says: "it is one thing to admit women into mankind and extend to them the rights of liberalism, it is another thing to challenge the humanist conceptions of man, woman and the nature of power and language" (Weedon 1997: 137).

From Bhutto's sun-kissed, unblemished smile to the mob-like female masses of the Lal Masjid, I have drawn attention to a whole realm of visual experience and practice that can barely be approached without attention to the elusive, fantastic, contingent, and the erotic. I have remained skeptical of the largely Western framing in which the corporeal is analyzed as a key modality of freedom, as the constitutive model to determine these subjects' liberatory or oppressed relations. The systemic, interdependent relationship between the implicit erotic heterosexuality of these photographic narratives and brown bodies as the new capital speaks to the dangerous state of a neocolonial apartheid that insists on difference (in oppression) while it contends that freedom is resolutely the same.

Each image—preeminent, hypnotic, fixating—recodes and reterritorializes the U.S. doctrine of Manifest Destiny. In all three visual cases, the erotics of empire tug readings of these women in at least two directions—toward an impossible idealized heterosexual femininity and towards its nightmarish opposite—utter degradation or utterly uncontrollable—conditions which pivot on simulations of aesthetics and embodiment. In chapter four, I trace how Benazir Bhutto's popularity and emblematic status in the American political scene imagines democracy from the vantage point of the hetero-erotic gaze, while in chapter three, Mukhtar Mai's unwillingness to embrace Western aesthetics troubles the hetero-erotic gaze even is it subjects her to its panoptical force. The female-led uprisings discussed in chapter five elude the tight assumptions of Pakistan's over-determining patriarchy even as these women rebels structure their resistance along hetero-erotic and national lines. Indeed, it is amazing how the public, largely U.S. driven discourse shifts from viewing these women as veiled victims of fundamentalist extremism to gender deviants. And in doing so, elide and dismiss the complexities of issues that face the formation of right-based discourses in Pakistan. Indeed, it is precisely because both white racism and white multiculturalism work at containing the increasing role and resistance of Pakistani women, and Muslim women broadly, that the very idea of the real Pakistani woman qualifies as a fantasy.

If scholars have identified visibility as a powerful form of governmentality that has becomes associated with a wide range of mechanisms of power, the concepts of security and sex are allied in this matrix. I recently came across the popular publication, *The Upstair's Wife: An Intimate History of Pakistan* (Rafia Zakaria, 2015), where Zakaria tells the story of her Aunt's forced polygamous marriage, capitalizing on a kind of accounting of Pakistani women that positions the nation-state (Pakistan) in binary opposition to international civil society. The praise following the novel's publication includes feminist columnist Katha Pollitt, feminist cultural critic Courtney Martin and feminist activist Medea Benjamin, cofounder of NGO Code Pink and author of *Drone Warfare*. Pollitt (2015) showers praises on the novel, saying "Zakaria tells two stories that are really the same story. One is the descent of Pakistan into violence, poverty, corruption, and extremist Islam; the other is the smoldering misery of family life in which women have little power, except, sometimes, over each other. *The Upstairs Wife* is a revelation." Courtney Martin, Award-winning Author of *Do It Anyway: The New Generation of Activists*, also showered praise on *The Upstairs Wife*, saying Zakaria "made me love the women there—their woundedness, their resilience, their uncertain future." Both reviews of the novel conflate the story of one woman with a tale of a total nation—where both are lain bare to the reader as wounded yet violent, powerless and uncertain, corrupt and manipulative.

Coda. Will the Real Pakistani Woman Please Stand Up?

The continued popularity of such stories on Pakistani women demonstrates that raced nations are narrativized through the *feminine racialized other*—here the story of one family's sordid transgressions stand in for the corruptive force of Pakistan itself. The "little power" women have "except over each other" that Pollitt speaks to is emblematic of a number of hetero-patriarchal societies including the U.S., insofar as dominant patriarchies always requires the complicity/participation of women, yet Pollitt expresses this "smoldering misery of family life" as unique to Pakistani women and as linked in an unclear way to the nation's "descent into violence, poverty, corruption, and extremist Islam." Like the *National Geographic* cover that mourns the soul of Pakistan using the exotic/erotic visuality of a woman, *The Upstairs Wife* is complicit in an ethnic and gendered mourning that politicizes, not the complexities of Pakistani women's lives and labor, but derives its politics from dark negotiations with the psychic pleasures of raced nations and bodies. Open and susceptible and deeply popular, the feminine, racialized body— here the Pakistani woman—is perfectly poised at the edge of the racial imagination and material history. She is the brown body *par excellence*— the body through which we come to know Pakistan, whose feminine resilience lines up with the great American fable of individual bootstraps, whose story unifies rather than exposes the repercussions of imperial sociality. Within the abstract circuit of capital, these stories become the only valid form of agency and aesthetics.

Randal Williams (2010) tells us that the influence of human rights on our cultural imaginary includes playing a critical role in providing the stories of abuse and violence, prescribing a framework for witnessing (both testimonial and spectatorial), structuring the modes of intelligibility (largely through psychoanalytic registers of trauma and healing and overdetermining the moral message. Similarly, I have always been drawn to Trinh Minh Ha's (1989:12) astute observation that "the imperial gaze loves the image of the native as a violated site." The figure of the Muslim *other* stands like a sentinel, marking the limits of West—the state system, human rights, civil freedom, democracy and even the basic expression of desirability, aesthetics and socialities.

Thus, alongside what Achilles Mbembe (2002) calls "deathworlds"— worlds of slow living death and dead living—there is also the creation of discursive spaces governed by forms of sovereignty that allow for specific survival/trauma stories that index the possibilities of a new democracy and those histories of colonization that claimed the superiority of the west. Foucault (1977:224) reminds us that, "the exercise of power is not a naked fact, an institutional right, nor is it a structure which holds out or is smashed: it is elaborated, transformed, organized; it endows itself with processes which are more or less adjusted to the situation." The language of liberal empowerment embedded in the fields I have analyzed inculcates and entitles the white racial state's interest in these women. The universalist embrace of woman as oppressed subject and brown as subject in need of civility should (although it often doesn't) raise questions about the subtle violence of visibility and visuality, the various ways visual culture expands the imperial lexicon, and how its global miredness enables and eroticizes violence against women. Instead we continue to think that images have a self-evident relationship to its object and that the particular economy, in which that image is produced, distributed and consumed is only marginally important. But images are very complicated and we must promote, in a mass sense, a visual literacy necessary to critically understand them.

Impossible Language, Complex Sights

At the heart of this book has been a key contemporary paradox of Orientalized visual culture: white (U.S.) fear mobilized to remember traumatized brown (Pakistani) bodies. But trauma, I would say, is fundamentally an anti-aesthetic and perhaps even, unrepresentable. It is, as Jacki Orr (2006), argues, "an impossible language, whose powers of communication remain secret, even to ourselves." So the question arises as to whether the visibility of trauma (and its most dominant form—visuality of traumatized bodies) can provide a way of acquiring power that doesn't engender the violence of colonial relations and the despotism of empire masked by the oppressed willed surrender to be visible? Do points of resistance inhabit the practice of visibility and visuality or is it surrender of another order? If it the latter is the case, then, we can see that the delineations of power are murky and uncertain. Therefore, what is at stake here is not maintaining the Pakistani woman as a real identitarian category, but rather examining these gendered visual formations in relation to colonial relations, the pleasure economy embedded in gazing at Pakistani women and the calculations of the global war.

As I stumbled upon image after image of Pakistan, I came to recognize that a critique of representation doesn't resolve the continuing

Coda. Will the Real Pakistani Woman Please Stand Up?

crisis of domination—coercive and consensual. The available critical vocabularies were failing to communicate the depth and intricacies of the dialectic of subjection and subjectivity, of domination and freedom, of being seen and being the subject of another's gaze. Of course, as Avery Gordon (2008:9) reminds us, "it is not simply the vocabularies themselves are at fault, but the constellation of effects, historical and institutional, that make a vocabulary a social practice of producing knowledge." Yes, it is important to remember, in fact, all the women in this project were or continue to be (e.g., Mukhtar Mai) subject to material violence in their political/public trajectories, in ways that are concealed and revealed by their visualities. But within forced environments of war, terrorism, national instability, and patriarchy, these women also deny their own frailty. In this way, visuality and making visible is not simply something that is done to these women (by Western/imperial others). It is something these women learn to manipulate and wield in their own interests. Moreover, it is important for us to begin to ponder how feminist activists in the local life-worlds of Pakistan negotiate these images and representations in their activism—activism that operates at both the level of and below the state.

But as signifiers of the charged complexity of Pakistani national identity, these visual subjects demonstrate ambiguous allegiance towards insurgent violence, gender and national boundaries. Hence, neither my queries nor my queering of these women produce a clear, consensual, and whole alternative. Rather my work encourages a rigorous vocabulary that deterritorializes established way of thinking and seeing (these women) and splits open the naturalization of the prevailing system of representation. Shifting the visual monolith from a single idiomatic discourse about the other to one that is perhaps more accurately framed as rhizomatic, extending tentacles and filaments through various points of power and pleasure (e.g., brown bodies, erotic violence and white hope) and ruptures the "truth" of sight, splintering into complexity. To rupture the "truth" of these representations opens a point of entry into unnamed, unidentified forms of freedom, a point around which a different kind of subjectivity might crystallize. The comfort, consolation, contentment, ease, and even enjoyment of these visual practices of and about Pakistan must be considered in this light.

Chapter Notes

Chapter One

1. The *niqab* is the proper term to describe these women's attire. It refers to the full body and face covering, incorrectly referred to as the veil both colloquially and within political realms, such as during the recent French controversial debated and throughout the media narrations of the Lal Masjid actors. I, however, use the term veil for this book to invoke its more politicized ideological contours and its dominant perception in the U.S. and Western visual and political culture. For the intellectual usefulness of this term, see Joan Wallach Scott (2007) *The Politics of the Veil*.

2. *Zenana* refers to the part of a house belonging to a Muslim family in South Asian countries, such as India and Pakistan, reserved for the women of the household.

3. The *niqab* refers to the face covering part of the burkha. *Niqabi*, a more colloquial term, refers to women who wear the *niqab*.

4. The female religious martyrs I speak about and analyze as a symbolic gender field are nameless, often spoken of or referred to as a group, a mass or a collective. It can possibly be argued, and indeed I do argue this in Chapter Five, that part of their radical resistance to advancing capitalism and U.S. imperialism is their refusal to be named. For an interesting discussion of naming and subject-hood, see Denise Riley (1988), *Am I That Name?*

5. The *niqab* or *hijab* has never been a common part of the Pakistani cultural repertoire. Instead, a *dupatta*, part of the Pakistani *Shalwar Kameez*, which loosely covers the hair and frames the face, is most commonly worn. Often, the *dupatta* is worn as a shawl, and/or only put over the hair during prayer, and depending on form of religious-cultural practice, in the company of men or public, or within sacred spaces, such as the mosque.

Chapter Two

1. For a more thorough critique of *National Geographic*, see Lutz and Collins, *Reading National Geographic* (1993).

2. The capture and assassination of Osama bin Laden by Navy SEALs was brought up with pride in an important speech on national security in May 2013. Obama hailed the operation but added

that it could not be the norm. The reason, he said, was that the risks were immense and the cost of US's relationship with Pakistan and the backlash among the Pakistani public over encroachment on their territory was severe. Nonetheless, the SEALs were ordered to fight their way out if apprehended. The full force of the U.S. military would have been used to extricate them. Pakistan has a powerful, well-trained military, highly protective of state sovereignty. It also has nuclear weapons, and Pakistani specialists are concerned about the possible penetration of their nuclear security system by jihadi elements. It is also no secret that the population has been embittered and radicalized by Washington's drone terror campaign and other policies. The Bin Laden raid could have led to nuclear annihilation.

3. A French word which derives from the verb *jouir* meaning to have pleasure in, to enjoy, to appreciate, to savour; with a secondary meaning, as in English, of having rights and pleasures.

Chapter Three

1. National Geographic, 1985
2. Asma Jahangir, one of the most well known public activists in Pakistan, is a founding member of The Human Rights Commission of Pakistan and the U.N. Special Rapporteur on extrajudicial killings.
3. My point of reference can be most quickly captured by the well-known feminist text, *Gyn/Ecology*, written by Mary Daly in 1978. In this radical feminist treatise, Daly relies on and reproduces a number of hackneyed stereotypes of the oppressed third world women, exacerbating the narrative that the West is the best. Hardly an antiquated argument, Susan Moller Okin (1998) rearticulated such a feminist position in her more liberal debates with postcolonial thinkers, in her book, *Is Multiculturalism Bad for Women?* More recent feminists' praise for anti–Islamic narratives, such as Katha Pollitt and Susan Sontag's hailing of *Reading Lolita in Tehran*, also speaks to the popularity of the position and the imperial impulse embedded in liberalism, hence liberal feminism.
4. BBC. 2005. "Gang Rape Victim's Police Problems." June 21. Available at http://news.bbc.co.uk/2/hi/south_asia/4114714.stm.
5. Of course, this eroticization of violence against the feminine, racialized *other* serves to simultaneously control and mitigate the fear of the violent brown/Muslim male. The *Newsweek* photograph discussed in chapter one captures this fear in a gross exaggeration of angry brown male bodies. To be sure, individuals who make military decisions have a fear of brown male bodies (indeed they may), but such fear, which is in circulation through imagery and text in the public sphere, comes in handy when they need to consolidate public opinion in support of military action in brown/black countries. In fact, in *Half the Sky's* film premiere, the expert speakers identify that part of the problem for women in the developing world is that "public space in the third world has the same atmosphere as, say, a men's locker room." In the best –selling book, *Half the Sky* (2010:45) Kristoff and Wudunn use the language "testosterone-heavy" to describe the public spaces of the third world. Even Kristoff's statement on Mai speaking out against her perpetrators, when he states: "It's difficult for people outside of this place to understand what kind of courage that took" regenerates the notion of brown masculinity as maliciously aligned against women's voices and women's (sexual) freedom (2005, *CBS Special Report*). Kristoff (237) also argues, "emancipation of women offers another dimension in which to tackle geopolitical challenges such as terrorism." Pointing to U.S. funding of money and weapon in Pakistani after 9/11 to help fight terrorism, which Kristoff argues, led to U.S. unpopularity, the Musharraf regime's instability and the extremists' popularity. "Imagine if we

Chapter Notes

had used the money instead to promote education and microfinance in rural Pakistan, through Pakistani organizations. The result would likely have been greater popularity for the United States and the greater involvement of women in society" (Kristoff 2009:237). Kristoff goes on to say that when women gain a voice in society, there's evidence of less violence. "After the Musharraf government collapsed in 2008, a cloud lifted from Mukhtar's operations, the intelligence agencies began to spy on terrorists instead of on Mukhtar" (79). By linking gender discrimination to national security, first world hegemony is not just glossed over, but strategically re-imagined and enshrined within the field of (brown) global human rights.

6. See, for example, Moon Charania, 2014, "Precarious Citizenship: Feminism, Sexuality and The Rhetoric of Westernization in Pakistan." In *Handbook on Gender in South Asia*, Leela Fernandez, ed. (London: Routledge), 318–332.

Chapter Four

1. Fanon (1963) in the *Wretched of the Earth* engages in a devastating treatise on violence in the colony, among the colonized.

2. The conversation actually took place in Urdu. The word used to describe Bhutto was *churi*, which literally translates to knife, as a means to imply how sharp, shrewd and intelligent she was but through a largely pejorative framing.

3. While Kierkegaard (1843) was one of the first in Western philosophical discourse to speak of beauty as a moral project, this idea has clearly been taken up by a number of theorists, such as bell hooks (1989), Patricia Hill Collins (2004) and, of course, can be traced through varying colonial trajectories.

4. I refer here to recent events in France where the *burqa* is being banned. For more on this, see *Time*, 3 May 2010 or *BBC*, 8 April 2010.

5. Of course, it is important to note that Aristotle's original formulation excluded both women and people of color. But according to popular liberal multicultural strategies, the solution to such racist and sexist exclusions is often to "add and stir."

6. For more on Pakistan political development and crisis, see Sadia Toor (2013), *State of Islam: Culture and Cold War Politics in Pakistan*.

Chapter Five

1. In a report by the United Nations, 2007 was described as "an exceptionally violent year in Pakistan, which saw sharp increases in violence carried out by Islamist extremists and by the state" (Report of the United Nations Commission of Inquiry into the facts and circumstances of the assassination of former Pakistani Prime Minister Mohtarma Benazir Bhutto, 16 April 2010), culminating in the assassination of Benazir Bhutto, on the 27th of December, 2007.

2. For a more detailed article on the role and relevance of Chinese sex workers in Pakistan, see *New York Times*, 12 July 2007.

3. By some accounts, the Chinese women were held for three days within the women quarters of the mosque (*GeoTV—Mere Mutabik*, translated, *In My Opinion*). But most American and British media accounts state the women were released the next day.

4. The "furor" over Muslim veiling practices in the secular West really depends on the type and style of veiling. In fact, some forms of veiling have been lauded, even romanticized, especially in recent years in American popular culture, as emancipatory signs and as a rejection of the monopolization of notions of "modernity" by secular Westerners. It is also important to acknowledge that secularism in the U.S. is not necessarily a dominant ideology, though secularist discourses often dominate the political landscape. In fact, as studies

Chapter Notes

acknowledge, the U.S. population tends to be religious, much more so than in Western Europe. With that mindset comes a whole new landscape of symbolic formations of emancipation and agency, where a simple "veiling = oppression" is increasingly challenged. Rather, political participation, education, fertility, marriage, legal rights, the proliferation of gender-based violence, etc. are the focus of most recent debates, while cultural practices like veiling are not seen in a wholly negative way anymore, even within the mainstream media.

5. The anthropological use of the notion "resistance" has been rightly criticized for underestimating the strength and diversity of power structures. See, for example, the article of Lila Abu-Lughod, 1990, "The Romance of Resistance," *American Ethnologist* 17(1).

Bibliography

Abu-Lughod, Lila. 2010. "The Active Social Life of Muslim Women's Rights: A Plea for Ethnography, Not Polemic, with Cases from Egypt and Palestine." *Journal of Middle East Women's Studies* 6 (1), Winter, 1–45.

Agamben, Giorgio. 2000. *Means Without Ends: Notes on Politics*. Minnesota: University of Minnesota Press.

Ahmed, Sara. 2010. *The Promise of Happiness*. Durham: Duke University Press.

Ajami, Faood. 2007. "With Us or Against Us." *Huffington Post*. January 7. Available at http://www.nytimes.com/2007/01/07/books/review/ajami.html?pagewanted=print&_r=0.

Al-Ali, Nadje. 2000. *Secularism, Gender and the State in the Middle East: The Egyptian Women's Movement*. Cambridge: Cambridge University Press.

Alexander, Jacqui. 2005. *Pedagogies of Crossing: Meditations on Feminism, Sexual Politics, Memory and the Sacred*. Durham: Duke University Press.

Anderson, Benedict. 1983. *Imagined Communities*. London: Verso.

Ang, Ien. 1982. *Watching Dallas: Soap Opera and the Melodramatic Imagination*. New York: Routledge.

Anzaldua, Gloria. 1987. *Borlerlands/La Frontera*. San Francisco: Spinxters Publishers.

Appadurai, Arjun. 1996. *Modernity at Large: Cultural Dimensions of Globalization*. Minnesota: University of Minnesota Press.

Asad, Talal. 2003. *Formations of the Secular: Christianity, Islam and Modernity*. Stanford: Stanford University Press.

Bacchetta, Paola. 1994. "Communal Property/Sexual Property: On Representations of Muslim Women in Hindu Nationalist Discourse." *Forging Identities: Gender, Communities, and the State*. New Delhi: Kali Press.

Badiou, Allain. 2002. *Ethics: An Essay on the Understanding of Evil*. London: Verso.

Bano, Masooda. 2009. "Are These Religious Schools Linked to Islamic Fundamentalism?" *BBC*. May 27. http://www.bbc.co.uk/radio4/womanshour/04/2009_21_wed.shtml.

Barthes, Roland. 1972. *Mythologies*. New York: Hill and Wang.

Barthes, Roland. 1981. *Camera Lucida:*

Bibliography

Reflections on Photography. New York: Hill and Wang.

Baudrillard, Jean. *Carnival and Cannibal: Ventriliqous Evil.* London: Seagull Books.

Baudry, Jean Louis. 1985. *The Ideological Effects of the Basic Cinematographic Apparatus; Narrative, Apparatus, Ideology: A Film Theory Reader.* New York: Columbia University Press.

BBC. 2005. "Gang Rape Victim's Police Problems." BBC.com. June 21. Available at http://news.bbc.co.uk/go/pr/fr/-/2/hi/south_asia/4114714.stm, Accessed June 2008.

BBC. 2007. "Mosque Survivor "Willing" to Die." BBC.com. July 19. http://news.bbc.co.uk/2/hi/south_asia/6907107.stm.

BBC. 2011. "Profile: Mukhtar Mai." April 21. Available at, http://www.bbc.co.uk/news/world-south-asia-13163169.

Berger, P., and Lockman, T. 1966. *The Social Construction of Reality: A Treatise in the Sociology of Knowledge.* New York: Anchor Books.

Bhabha, Homi. 1994. *The Location of Culture.* New York: Routledge.

Bhattercharyya, Gargi. 2008. *Dangerous Brown Men: Exploiting Sex, Violence and Feminism in the Global War.* London: Zed Books.

Boehmer, Elleke. 2005. *Stories of Women: Gender and Narrative in the Postcolonial Nation.* Manchester: Manchester University Press.

Bordo, Susan. 2004. *Unbearable Weight: Feminism, Western Culture and the Body.* Berkeley: University of California Press.

Bourdieu, Pierre. 1998. *Practical Reason: On the Theory of Action.* California: Stanford Press.

Britzman, Deborah. 2005. "Is There a Queer Pedagogy?—Or Stop Reading Straight?" *Educational Theory,* 42: 151–165.

Brown, Wendy. 2005. *Edgework: Critical Essays on Knowledge and Politics.* Princeton, NJ: Princeton University Press.

Butler, Judith. 1993. *Bodies That Matter: On the Discursive Limits of "Sex."* New York: Routledge.

Butler, Judith. 2004. *Precarious Life: The Powers of Mourning and Violence.* London: Verso.

Chakrabarty, Dipesh. 2002. *Habitations of Modernity.* Chicago: Chicago University Press.

Chatterjee, Partha. 1993. *The Nation and Its Fragments: Colonial and Postcolonial Histories.* Princeton, NJ: Princeton University Press.

Chomsky, Noam. 2003. *Hegemony or Survival: America's Quest for Global Domination.* New York: Owl Books.

Clifford, James. 2010. *Writing Culture: The Poetics and Politics of Ethnography.* Berkeley: University of California Press.

CNN. 2007. "Bhutto Took Risks in Life." December 27. Available at http://www.cnn.com/2007/WORLD/asiapcf/12/27/bhutto.obit/.

Collingham, E.M. 2001. *Imperial Bodies.* Cambridge: Polity Press.

Dalwymple, William. 2007. "Letter from Pakistan." *New Yorker.* July 23. Available at http://www.newyorker.com/reporting/2007/07/23/070723fa_fact_dalrymple.

Dean, Jodi. 2009. *Democracy and Other Neoliberal Fantasies.* Durham: Duke University Press.

De Beauvoir, Simone. 1949/2011. *The Second Sex.* New York: Vintage Books.

De Lauretis, Teresa. 1987. *Technologies of Gender: Essays on Theory, Film and Fiction.* Bloomington: Indiana University Press.

Deleuze, Gilles, and Gauttari, Felix. 1987. *Thousand Plateaus: Capitalism and Schizophrenia.* Minnesota: University of Minnesota Press:.

Derrida, Jacques. *Of Grammatology.* Baltimore: Johns Hopkins University Press.

Dougary, Ginny. 2010. "Destiny's Daughter." *Huffington Post.* January 24. Available at http://www.huffingtonpost.com/ginny-dougary/destinys-daughter_b_434530.html. Accessed February 23, 2014.

Eisenstein, Zillah. 1998. *Global Obscen-*

Bibliography

ities: Patriarchy, Capitalism and the Lure of Cyberfantasy. New York: New York University Press.

Eisenstein, Zillah. 2007. *Sexual Decoys*. New York: Routledge.

Enloe, Cynthia. 2004. *The Curious Feminist: Searching for Women in a New Age of Empire*. Berkeley: University of California Press.

Esteva, Gustavo, and Prakash, Madhu Suri. 1998. *Grassroots and Postmodernism*. London: Zed Books.

Faludi, Susan. 2007. *The Terror Dream*. New York: Metropolitan Books.

Fanon, Frantz. 1963. *Wretched of the Earth*. New York: Grove Press.

Fanon, Frantz. 1967. *Black Skin, White Masks*. New York: Grove Press.

Fernandes, Leela. 2013.*Transnational Feminism in the United States: Knowledge, Ethics, Power*. New York: New York University Press.

Foucault, Michel. 1977. *Discipline and Punish: The Birth of the Prison*. London: Penguin Books.

Foucault, Michel. 1978/1990. *The History of Sexuality: Volume I*. New York: Vintage Books.

Foucault, Michel. 1997. *The Hermeneutics of the Subject: Lectures at College De France, 1977–78*. New York: Picador.

Foucault, Michel. 1997. *Security, Territory, Population: Lectures at College De France, 1975–76*. New York: Picador.

Foucault, Michel. 1997. *Society Must Be Defended: Lectures at College De France, 1975–76*. New York: Picador.

French, Howard. 2007. "Letter from China: Mosque Siege Reveals Chinese Connection." *New York Times*. July 12. Available at http://www.nytimes.com/2007/07/12/world/asia/12iht-letter.1.6629789.html.

Gopinath, Gayatri. 2005. *Impossible Desires: Queer Diasporas and South Asian Public Cultures*. Durham: Duke University Press.

Gordon, Avery. 2008. *Ghostly Matters: Haunting and the Sociological Imagination*. Minneapolis: University of Minnesota Press.

Gorenfield, John. 2010. "With Its Horrifying Cover Story, Time Gave the War a Boost. Did Its Reporter Profit?" *Observer*. August 12. Available at http://observer.com/2010/08/with-its-horrifying-cover-story-itimei-gave-the-war-a-boost-did-its-report er-profit/. Accessed on, October 4, 2013.

Grewal, Inderpal. 2005. *Transnational America: Feminisms, Diasporas, Neoliberalisms*. Durham: Duke University Press.

Grewal, Inderpal, and Caren Kaplan. 1994. *Scattered Hegemonies: Postmodernity and Transnational Feminist Practice*. Minneapolis: University of Minnesota Press.

Grosz, Elizabeth. 1994. *Volatile Bodies: Towards a Corporeal Feminism*. Bloomington: Indiana University Press.

Guha, R., and Spivak, G. 1988. *Selected Subaltern Essays*. London: Oxford University Press.

Hage, Ghassen. 2003. *Against Paranoid Nationalism: Searching for Hope in a Shrinking Society*. Sydney: Pluto Press.

Hall, Stuart. 1997. *Representation: Cultural Representations and Signifying Practices*. London: Open University.

Hartmaan, Saadiya. 2007. *Lose Your Mother: Journey Along the Trans Atlantic Slave Trade*. New York: Farrar, Straus and Giroux.

Hassan, Syed. 2007. "Profile: Islamabad's Red Mosque." *BBC*. 27 July. Available at http://news.bbc.co.uk/2/hi/south_asia/6503477.stm.

Heidegger, M. 1977. "The Age of the World Picture." In Lovitt, W., ed., *The Question Concerning Technology and Other Essays*. New York: Harper and Row.

Hoodbhoy, Pervez. 2007. "What Does the Lal Masjid Mosque Siege Tell Us About the Growth of Extremism in Pakistan?" *Prospect*. July 28. Available at http://www.prospectmagazine.co.uk/magazine/afterlalmasjid/.

Husain, Irfan. 2007. "Reaping What We Sowed." Dawnwww. April 14. Available at http://archives.dawn.com/

Bibliography

weekly/mazdak/20070414.htm, accessed June 2013.

Hyat, Kamila. 2007. "Jamia Hafsa: A Window into the Soul of Pakistan's Madrassah Underworld." Shirkat Gah Publication, http://www.shirkatgah.org/publications/Special-Bulletin-2007-05-18.pdf, accessed June 2010.

Irigiray, Luce. 1985. *The Sex Which Is Not One.* Ithaca, NY: Cornell University Press.

Jamal, Amina. 2005. "Transnational Feminism as Critical Practice: A Reading of Feminist Discourses in Pakistan." *Meridians: Feminism, Race, Transnationalism* 5(2): 5782.

Jameson, Frederick. 1981. *The Political Unconscious.* Ithaca, NY: Cornell University Press.

Janmohammed, Abdul. 1985. "The Economy of Manichean Allegory: The Function of Racial Difference in Colonialist Literature." *Critical Inquiry* (12:1), Autumn: 5987.

Jarmakani, Amira. 2008. *Imagining Arab Womanhood: The Cultural Mythology of Veils, Harems and Belly Dancers in the U.S.* New York: Palgrave Macmillan.

Jeffrey, Patricia, and Basu, Amrita. 1998. *Appropriating Gender: Women's Activism and Politicized Religion in South Asia.* New York: Routledge.

Jones, Amelia. 2003. *Feminism and Visual Culture.* New York: Routledge.

Jussim, Estelle. 1984. *The Eternal Moment: Essays on Photographic Representation.* New York: Aperture Foundation.

Kandiyoti, Deniz. 1991. *Women, Islam and the State.* Philadelphia: Temple University Press.

Kelley, Bayes, and Hawkesworth. 2001. *Gender, Globalization, and Democratization.* Lanham, MD: Rowman and Littlefield.

Khan, Fawzia. 2007. "Betwixt and Between? Women, the Nation and Islamization in Pakistan." *Social Identities* 13(1): 1929.

Khan, Khalid Hasan. 2007. "Revolution or What?" Dawnwww. April 29. Available at http://archives.dawn.com/weekly/dmag/archive/070429/dmag4.htm, accessed June 2013.

Khan, Shahnaz. 2001. "Between Here and There Feminist Solidarity and Afghan Women." Blog, Winter, http://genders.org/33/2001.

Khan, Shahnaz. 2007. *Zina, Transnational Feminism and the Moral Regulation of Pakistani Women.* London: Oxford University Press.

Koehler, Robert. 2011. "The Hilary Nutcracker." *Huffington Post.* May 25. Available at http://www.huffingtonpost.com/robert-koehler/the-hillary-nutcracker_b_87779.html.

Kristoff, Nicholas, and Wudunn, Sheryl. 2009. *Half the Sky: Turning Oppression into Opportunity for Women Worldwide.* New York: Knopf.

Lacan, Jacques. 1992. *The Ethics of Psychoanalysis, 19591970.* Paris: Le Edition.

Landau, Paul, and Kaspin, Deborah. 2002. *Images and Empires: Visuality in Colonial and Postcolonial Africa.* Berkeley: University of California Press.

Lutz, Catherine, and Collins, Jane. 1993. *Reading National Geographic.* Chicago: University of Chicago Press.

Mbembe, Achille. 2003. "Necropolitics." *Public Culture* 15(1): 11–40.

McClintock, Ann. 1995. *Imperial Leather: Race, Gender and Sexuality in the Colonial Contest.* New York: Routledge.

McClintock, Ann. 2009. "Paranoid Empires: Specters from Guantanamo and Abu Ghraib." *Small Axe* 13(1): 51–74.

McRobbie, Angela. 2008. *The Aftermath of Feminism: Gender, Culture and Social Change.* London: Sage Publications.

Memmi, Albert. 1965. *The Colonizer and the Colonized.* Boston: Beacon Press.

Mennon, Madhavi. 2011. *Shakesqueer.* Durham: Duke University Press.

Mernissi, Fatema. 2005. *Islam and Democracy: Fear of the Modern World.* London: Basic Books.

Miller, Francis Taylor. 1911. *The Photo-*

graphic *History of the Civil War.* Springfield, MA: Patriot Publishing.

Minh-Ha, Trinh. 1989. *Woman, Native, Other: Writing Postcoloniality and Feminism.* Bloomington: Indiana University Press.

Mirzoeff, Nicholas. 1998. *The Visual Culture Reader,* 2d ed. New York: Routledge.

Moghadam, Valentine. 1994. *Gender and National Identity: Women and Politics in Muslim Societies:* London: Zed Books.

Mohanty, Chandra Talpade. 2003. *Feminism Without Borders: Decolonizing Theory, Practicing Solidarity.* Durham: Duke University Press.

Moreau, Jon. 2007. "Where the Jihad Lives Now." *Newsweek.* October 20. Available at http://www.thedailybeast.com/newsweek/2007/10/20/where-the-jihad-lives-now.html.

Morrison, Toni. 1982. *Sula.* New York: Plume Printing.

Mulvey, Laura. 1989. *Visual and Other Pleasures.* Bloomington: University of Indiana Press.

Naber, Nadine. 2006. "Arab-American Femininities: Beyond Arab Virgin/American(Ized) Whore." *Feminist Studies* (32): 87–107.

Narayan, Uma. 1997. *Dislocating Cultures: Identities, Traditions, and Third World Feminisms.* New York: Routledge.

National Geographic. 2007. "Struggle for the Soul of Pakistan." September.

Newsweek. 2008. "The Most Dangerous Place on Earth Isn't Iraq. It's Pakistan." October 29.

Okin, Susan Moller. 1999. *Is Multiculturalism Bad for Women?* Princeton, NJ: Princeton University Press.

Pierce, Steven, and Rao, Anupama. 2006. *Discipline and the Other Body: Correction, Corporeality, Colonialism.* Durham: Duke University Press.

Pine-Coffin, R.S. 1961. *The Confessions.* Middlesex: Penguin Press.

Pinney, Christopher, and Peterson, Nicholas. 2003. *Photography's Other History.* Durham: Duke University Press.

Puar, Jasbir. 2007. *Terrorist Assemblages: Homonationalism in Queer Times.* Durham: Duke University Press.

Ranciere, Jacques. 2013. *The Politics of Aesthetics.* London: Bloomsbury.

Rich, Adrienne. 1980. "Compulsary Heterosexuality and Lesbian Existence." *Signs* (5): 631–657.

Rose, Gillian. 2007. *Visual Methodologies.* London: Sage Publications.

Rose, Nicholas. 1989. *Governing the Soul: The Shaping of the Private Self.* New York: Free Association Books.

Rowland, Debran. 2002. *Boundaries of Her Body: The Troubling History of Women's Rights in America.* New York: Sphynx Publishing.

Said, Edward. 1979. *Orientalism.* New York: Vintage Books.

Sangari, KumKum. 1999. *Politics of the Possible: Essays on Gender, History, Narratives, Colonial English.* New Delhi: Tulika.

Scott, Joan Wallach. 2007. *The Politics of the Veil.* Princeton, NJ: Princeton University Press.

Sengupta, Somini. 2007. "Red Mosque Fueled Islamic Fire in Young Women." *New York Times.* July 24. Available at http://www.nytimes.com/2007/07/24/world/asia/24madrasa.html?_r=1&oref=slogin.

Shahid. D. 2007. "Women of Lal Masjid." *Geotv.* May 21. Available at http://www.youtube.com/watch?v=H1TC2VC5mEg.

Sharify-Funk, Meena. 2008. *Encountering the Transnational: Women, Islam and the Politics of Interpretation.* Burlington, VT: Ashgate.

Sharma, Parvez. 2011. "The Martyrdom of Benazir Bhutto." *Huffington Post.* May 25. Available at http://www.huffingtonpost.com/parvez-sharma/the-martyrdom-of-benazir-_b_79560.html.

Shohat, Ella. 2001. *Talking Visions: Multicultural Feminism in a Transnational Age.* Cambridge: Massachusetts Institute of Technology Press.

Sjoberg, Laura, and Gentry, Caron. 2007. *Mothers, Monsters, Whores:*

Bibliography

Women's Violence in the Global Politics. London: Zed Books.

Sontag, Susan. 2003. *Regarding the Pain of Others*. New York: Picador.

Spivak, Gayatri. 1988. "Can the Subaltern Speak?" In Cary Nelson and Lawrence Grossberg, eds., *Marxism and the Interpretation of Culture*, 271–317.

Stan, Adele. 2007. "Benazir Bhutto: An Imperfect Feminist." *The American Prospect*. December 31. Available at http://prospect.org/article/benazir-bhutto-imperfect-feminist.

Tagg, John. 1988. *Burden of Representation: Essays on Photographies and History*. Minneapolis: University of Minnesota Press.

Tausig, Michael. 1999. *Defacement: Public Secrecy and the Labor of the Negative*. Stanford: Stanford University Press.

Time. 2010. "What Happens If We Leave Afghanistan." August 9.

Walkerdine, Valerie. 1997. *Daddy's Girl: Young Girls and Popular Culture*. Cambridge, MA: Harvard University Press.

Weedon, Chris. 1997. *Feminist Practice and Poststructuralist Theory*. London: Blackwell Press.

Weiss, Anita M. 2003. "Interpreting Islam and Women's Rights: Implementing CEDAW in Pakistan." *International Sociology* (18): 581–60.

Williams, Randall. 2010. *The Divided World: Human Rights and Its Violence*. Minneapolis: University of Minnesota Press.

Zia, Afiya. 2008. "The Reinvention of Feminism in Pakistan." Veiwpointonline.net. July 9. Available at http://www.viewpointonline.net/Old/fullstory.php?t=The%20reinvention%20of%20feminism%20in%20Pakistan&f=full-9-july-16.php&y=2010&m=july, accessed June 2013.

Zita, Jacqueline. 1998. *Body Talk: Philosophical Reflections on Sex and Gender*. New York: Columbia University Press.

Žižek, Slavoj. 2008. *Violence*. New York: Picador.

Žižek, Slavoj. 2012. "Zero Dark Thirty: Hollywood's Gift to American Power." *The Guardian*, January 25. Available at http://www.dailymail.co.uk/tvshowbiz/reviews/article-2267854/Zero-Dark-Thirty-review-Oscar-favourite-torture-watch-subtle-Die-Hard.html#ixzz2PDTbSH53.

Index

Abu Dhabi 7–9, 11
Abu Ghraib 38–40, 66
affect 3, 5, 13, 20, 29, 64, 86, 127, 130
Ahmed, Sara 19, 128
Aisha Bibi 24, 42, 60–62, 65–67
Algeria 110–112, 123
amnesia 25; historical 101; racial 125
Asad, Talal 24, 56, 126
authenticity 4, 49, 78, 85, 97, 129–130

BBC 17, 47–49, 52, 73–74, 79, 86, 101, 109, 114–115, 117, 123
beauty 65–66, 76–77, 79, 81, 83–85, 87, 92, 102, 106
Beijing 104–105
Benazir Bhutto 13, 21–22, 25, 53, 55–57, 71–107, 109, 117, 131–132; *Bhutto: The Film* 17, 99
brown 23, 27, 33, 40, 46, 70, 79, 100, 104; bodies 2, 20, 30, 38, 41, 44, 61–62, 64, 83, 130–133, 135; female other/subject 14–16, 26, 32, 42–43, 85, 90, 96, 134; men/male 10–11, 35–36, 69, 87, 97–99; women/girls 9, 12, 14, 17, 21–22, 24, 29, 31, 37, 45, 53, 56–59, 66–67, 69, 80, 113
Bush, Laura 48, 53, 116; Axis of Evil 61, 100

China 108; prostitutes 125, 126
class 4, 21, 22, 30, 31, 37, 39, 66, 70, 77, 79, 80, 81, 84–88, 90, 92–94, 97–98, 104

Clifford, James 4, 63, 92
Clinton, Hillary 93
CNN 58, 97
colonialism 4, 11, 14, 15, 25, 29, 30, 32, 35, 48, 53, 59, 61–62, 68–69, 72, 79, 83, 87, 91, 93, 98, 100–101, 105, 110–113, 115, 119, 121–123, 130–131, 134; 93, 110, 113, 121; neocolonialism 12, 22, 37, 43, 61, 66, 76, 118, 122, 124; postcolonialism 2, 5, 13, 14, 31, 33, 44–45, 51, 84, 86, 104–105
cultural studies 4, 15

Dalí, Salvador 71
Deleuze, Gilles 122, 130
democracy 14, 22–25, 33–34, 36–37, 40, 71, 73–81, 83–85, 87–94, 97, 99–107, 131, 133; democratization 13, 80
desire 1–3, 9–16, 19–20, 25–26, 30–32, 35, 37–40, 42, 49, 52–53, 61–65, 74, 76, 81, 84–85, 87–88, 91, 93, 96, 101, 106, 108–110, 115–116, 122, 126, 133–135, 138

Economist 34–35, 97
education 50, 62, 81, 103–104; girls' 43, 68–70; Pakistani 30
empire 12, 14, 17, 23–25, 27, 32, 37–40, 52, 59, 67, 70, 74, 77–81, 85, 87–88, 92, 94, 100, 102–103, 107, 111–112, 118, 121, 123, 125, 131, 134
English 1, 24, 99, 117, 124, 138, 145
eroticism 5, 9, 10–15, 19, 24, 30, 38, 40,

147

Index

42–43, 61–67, 76, 79, 81, 90–91, 98, 100, 109–110, 113, 117–118, 127; hetero-eroticism 5, 11, 14, 19, 25, 67, 71, 76, 79, 80, 84, 90, 92, 103–106, 115–116, 118

Fanon 4, 16, 31, 52, 72, 104–105, 111–113, 122–123
femininity 9–10, 20–22, 30, 33, 65, 81, 84–85, 88, 90, 93, 117, 122, 131; Muslim 115, 118; Pakistani 30, 88
feminism 2–5, 8, 10–12, 14–15, 19–23, 25–26, 31–33, 37, 44, 47–48, 64, 68, 70, 74–75, 80, 88, 93, 104–105, 132; faux 9; liberal 12–13, 32, 37; postcolonial 40, 47, 55–56, 67–69, 72–73, 112, 122, 124–125, 128, 130, 135; western 45; white 39
Foucault, Michel 4, 18, 38–39, 52, 56, 61–62, 75, 80, 106, 110, 118, 134
France 8, 32, 38, 39, 48, 61, 92, 105, 110–112, 137–139

gender 5, 9, 12, 20, 23, 25, 32, 37, 40, 44, 45, 58, 61, 66, 70, 78–79, 85, 88, 92–95, 98, 104, 105, 109, 118, 121, 123, 126, 132, 135, 137, 139–141; gendered 3–4, 10, 16–17, 21–22, 31, 33–34, 39, 41, 43, 50, 69, 96, 106–107, 111–112, 119, 120, 125, 127, 130–131, 133, 134; gendering 18, 113
Germany 111
global war *see* war
Grewal, Inderpal 14, 22, 33, 41, 44–45, 51, 91

Half the Sky 17, 42, 47, 51, 57–59
Hall, Stuart 15, 51
heterosexuality 13, 36, 63, 78, 80, 107, 120, 128, 131; heteroerotic 5, 11, 14, 67, 76, 84, 92, 106, 115–116, 118, 132
Hollywood 12, 36, 48, 58
human rights 13–14, 22–24, 36–37, 40–45, 47–50, 52–55, 62, 66–67, 69–70, 90, 92, 96, 100, 105, 131, 133, 138

imperialism 4, 15, 37–38, 44, 70, 100
India 17, 29, 36, 73, 83–84, 110–111, 116, 137
invisibility 37, 50, 54, 126–127
Islam 2, 11, 14, 16, 22, 27, 27, 55, 68, 90, 96–98, 104, 122, 131, 132
Islamabad, Pakistan 13, 25, 36, 108, 125
Islamic/Islamist 30, 32, 53, 92, 95, 99–100, 109, 114, 117–118, 120–122; Islamization 73; Islamophobia 33–34, 38, 69

Jahangir, Asma 47, 54

Karachi 1–2, 69, 71–72, 89, 95
Kristof, Nicholas 17, 33, 48, 51–52, 55, 57, 59, 63, 111

Lacan, Jacques 40, 49
Lahore 1, 47, 71, 76, 77
Lal Masjid 13, 22, 25, 39, 88, 93, 108–127, 131
liberal 59, 73–74, 103, 117, 121, 124; discourse 40; empowerment 134; ethos 39; feminism 11–13, 32, 37, 55, 106; gaze 48; humanism 44, 104–105, 110, 113, 122; ideology 50

Malala Yousafzai 16, 43–44, 50, 56–57, 60, 67–70, 130
Marisa Tomei 58–59
martyrs 13, 22, 25, 88, 92–93, 109–110, 112–113, 117, 122–123, 125–127
masculinity 19, 23, 112, 120, 138; brown 96; Muslim 2, 36; Occidental 35
media 16–17, 25, 38, 42–43, 51, 61–62, 64, 68–70, 74, 79, 83, 89, 97, 104, 106, 109–110, 114–120, 124, 126
misogyny 4, 67, 105
Mukhtar Mai 13, 20–22, 24, 27, 42–44, 46–59, 61–69, 91, 93, 102, 109, 132, 135
Mulvey, Laura 16, 31, 30, 62, 65, 76, 119
Musharraf, Pervez 33, 47–48, 51, 53–54, 73, 76, 93, 96–97, 108, 117
Muslim 2, 9–17, 20, 22–23, 25, 31–45, 47–49, 55–56, 61–63, 68–69, 73, 75, 84, 97–98, 105, 109–120, 122–123, 127, 129, 132

nation-state 32–33, 60, 111; Muslim 62; Pakistani 24, 29, 52, 107, 125, 130, 132; United States 39, 91
National Geographic 27–30, 32, 36, 40, 44, 57, 60, 112, 133
nationalism 3, 12, 15, 23, 52; heteronationalism 126; homonationalism 39; Islamic 100, 122; Pakistani 77; third world 33; U.S. 17, 103, 120
New York Times 17, 43, 46–49, 56, 58, 63, 67, 79, 83, 85, 96, 115–116
Newsweek 17, 33, 35, 116

occidentalism 9, 35
Orient 75–76, 91, 106; Orientalism 11–12, 29, 38, 44, 48, 90, 97–98, 103, 116, 119, 134

paranoia 9, 15, 25, 34–35, 37–38, 42, 44, 60, 61, 66, 67, 109–111; empires 4, 15,

148

Index

38, 42, 48, 54, 59, 100; gaze 5; violence 26
photography 13, 19, 24, 30, 57, 67; human rights 24, 41, 67; postcolonial 51
pleasure *see* desire
psychoanalysis 40, 133

queerness 3–5, 14–15, 19–21, 24–25, 38, 70–71, 73–75, 77, 79, 81, 83, 85, 87, 89, 91, 93, 97, 101, 103–107, 110, 119–123, 128, 135

race 2, 4, 14, 17, 21, 24, 26, 30–33, 38–41, 57, 59, 64, 66, 78, 90, 92–94, 98, 104, 113, 127, 131
racism 10, 12, 14, 16, 20, 22, 26, 30–31, 33, 35, 37, 39, 41–43, 63, 67, 70, 84, 86, 88, 91, 124, 129–132, 134
Red Mosque *see* Lal Masjid
revolutionary 56, 112
romanticism 2, 43, 65, 99, 114

Said, Edward 15, 31, 35
Sex and the City 2 (SATC2) 7, 9–13, 18, 22, 29, 32, 36–38, 40, 43–44, 59, 80, 91, 98
sexuality 11, 13, 19–20, 22, 24, 31–33, 38–41, 57, 66, 69, 94, 106–107, 118–119; heterosexuality 120, 128, 131; sexualization 5, 10, 14, 17, 30, 32, 39, 59, 63, 67, 80–81, 91, 93, 111–113, 125–127
Shazia Khalid 53–55
Sontag, Susan 41, 50
spectatorship 103; American 60; Suburban 51
subaltern 2, 104–105, 113, 121

television 68, 72
terrorism 2, 13, 14, 17, 23, 25–26, 34–36, 38–39, 44, 60, 61, 92–95, 109, 113, 116, 118, 123, 127
Time 42, 59, 65, 79–80, 102
transnationalism 3–4, 14, 19, 22, 33, 37, 41, 49, 61, 84, 125

United States 10–14, 16–17, 19–20, 24–25, 29, 31–36, 39, 42–44, 47–48, 50–53, 57, 60–62, 65–70, 72–75, 80, 85, 90, 92, 99, 109, 111–112, 120, 125, 131–134; exceptionalism 2, 22; state/gaze 4, 23, 38, 54, 110
Urdu 2, 6, 24, 123, 139

veil 7–10, 12, 25, 39, 44, 91–92, 101, 109–117, 119, 122, 124–126, 132
violence 5, 7, 10, 19, 23, 35–36, 38–39, 48, 55, 60, 65, 70, 72–72, 98, 122–124, 126, 129–135; against women 45, 63, 67–68, 134, 127; anti–American 109; colonial 100–101, 110, 112; eroticized 64; imperial 4; sexual/gender 47, 66, 69
visibility 4, 10, 15, 53, 59, 64, 103, 105, 109, 111, 123–124; American 32, 52; hyper 14, 31, 54, 92, 131–132; Pakistan 33, 130; politics of 18–20, 25, 39, 50; regimes of 67, 126, 134; Western 55
visuality 5, 11, 16, 18–19, 24, 27, 29–30, 38, 39, 44, 50, 51, 59, 61, 64, 67, 75, 78–79, 80, 98, 101, 104–105, 110, 131, 133–135; American 53; culture 3, 10, 12, 15–16, 23–25, 31, 33–34, 41, 74, 128–130, 134; subject 22, 56, 100; technology 3, 117; voyeurism 31, 62, 85, 98, 102, 103, 127

war 1, 3, 4, 12, 20, 26, 27, 34, 36–38, 60–65, 73, 80, 93, 99, 111–113, 116, 130–132, 134–135; Cold War 123; global war 13, 14, 16, 24, 33, 35, 40, 44, 51, 127; machines 23
war-on-terror *see* war
whiteness 1–2, 9–12, 25, 30–32, 36–37, 39, 42–43, 52, 55, 57–58, 62–63, 66–67, 69–70, 76, 80, 83, 85–87, 90, 93–94, 98, 100–101, 104, 115, 120, 124–125, 129–130, 132, 134–135
Williams, Randall 24, 36, 41, 43–44, 53, 56, 78, 100, 110, 133
Woineshet 58–59, 62
Wudunn, Sheryl *see* Kristof, Nicholas

Zero Dark Thirty 36–37

149

www.ingramcontent.com/pod-product-compliance
Ingram Content Group UK Ltd.
Pitfield, Milton Keynes, MK11 3LW, UK
UKHW021846140426
5217IPUK00022B/1624